BASTARD QUEEN

BASTARD QUEEN

by

DOROTHY BENHAM

A Family Secret Revealed

Briton Publishing, LLC

BRITON
PUBLISHING

810 Eastgate North Drive, Suite 200
Cincinnati, OH 45245

www.britonpublishing.com

Copyright © 2021

All rights reserved.

No part of this publication may be reproduced in any form, or by any means, electronic or mechanical, including photocopying, recording, or any information browsing, storage, or retrieval system, without permission from Briton Publishing.

ISBN: 978-1-956216-00-4 (Hardcover)

Published by Briton Publishing

THE BASTARD QUEEN

Illegitimate child ... love child ... nullius filius ... bend sinister ... by-blow ... bar sinister ... whoreson ... out-of-wedlock child ... fruit of adultery ... natural child ... spurious offspring ... Miss America ... wait ... whaaaaa?

SISU

That ineffable spirit or inner fire that Finns call upon when all strength seems spent. Because of Sisu, we (Finns) find it possible to do almost anything except betray our honor or compromise our ideals. Sisu is extraordinary endurance.

CONTENTS

- ACKNOWLEDGMENTS 13
- OVERTURE 15
  - PERFECTION 17
  - SISU 19
- CHARACTERS 21
  - MARY DOROTHY ELEANOR TUOMI 21
  - ARCHIBALD BENHAM 25
- ACT ONE 33
  - SCENE 1: EARLY CHILDHOOD 33
  - SCENE 2: JR. HIGH 37
  - SCENE 3: HIGH SCHOOL 41
  - SCENE 4: COLLEGE 49
- ACT TWO 63
  - SCENE 1: THE JOURNEY BEGINS 63
  - SCENE 2: MISS MINNESOTA 67
  - SCENE 3: MISS AMERICA 75
- ACT THREE 121
  - MARRIAGES / CHILDREN / PERFORMANCES 121
- FINALE 145
  - SCENE 1: SHE'S GONE 145
  - SCENE 2: WHAT BABY? 151
  - SCENE 3: WHO KNEW? 155
  - SCENE 4: DNA 159
- ABOUT THE AUTHOR 175

ACKNOWLEDGMENTS

Because of loving contributions by family and friends, my story came to life with their memories brimming with honesty and without judgement. Some who carried the secret for many years and others who suspected.

Beverly Benham, Amber (Benham) Bodell Goetsch, Totiana (Benham) Pillsbury, Archibald Kelley Benham, Kilyn (Benham) Roth.

To my new friend Charles Shipman. Thank you. Thank you for being a best friend to Gary and Daryl and answering and allowing me to ask many questions over the last year shedding new light into my life.

Thank you to the fabulous team at Briton Publishing. Tony Moore, Rob Lowe, and editor extraordinaire Brinka Rauh who through this journey made it easy because of your expertise and humor. Thank you for laughing with me!

To my multi-talented friend Vicki Kueppers for helping with the cover design. Over the decades I have been able to count on you for last-minute music arrangements, videos, photos, and now a book design and format. Thank you. I treasure our friendship.

But most of all to Luis Perez who was with me when I learned of this news. Who has been my champion, remained by my side with loving encouragement, support, guidance, and who probably has this entire manuscript memorized! The depth of gratitude and love I have for you is beyond words.

OVERTURE

"The winner ... of a $15,000. 00 scholarship ... Miss America 1977 ... Dorothy Benham, Miss Minnesota!"

September 11, 1976

Twenty years old and my life was about to change forever. I was on to a new adventure, not knowing exactly what all it would encompass. I had put myself in the position to be plucked out of my comfort zone as a college student in the mid-west, and placed on the front page of newspapers all over the world. Into the middle of celebrity with people curious about me ... their new Miss America. So many questions about myself, my upbringing, family, beliefs, ideas. You name it; they asked it. The year took hold fast and was a constant, exhilarating whirlwind. Traveling twenty thousand miles a month with appearances and interviews every day, some on the tarmac as soon as you exited the plane. I grew an exorbitant amount that year, all while trying to not look like a deer in headlights. I never embraced the idea of being interviewed and to this day I don't enjoy them, believing it's because there is always a question that provokes my wondering, who am I?

The gravity of winning and questioning why, out of eighty-thousand contestants a year, was this title bestowed upon me? I may never fully understand. Luck perhaps? Fate? What I did know was I could do this for a year, make the most of it and just enjoy! For one year I would be Miss America 1977 only to realize, many years later, **once Miss America ... always Miss America ...** but still wondering ... *who is Dorothy Kathleen Benham?*

PERFECTION

Dorothy, you need more lipstick on; you look peak-ed add some blush, your hair could be highlighted, you're better as a blonde, you didn't sing well; you look tired; you may lose your shape after having a child; your bust is no longer firm; round and beautiful; they used to be so beautiful; your figure may be better after this last pregnancy-- your hips are rounder (they didn't stay rounder). Good Lord, that was after three children!

In her own way, mother meant well, but I always knew she was living through me and I let her and why not? It's much more fun to share achievements with someone else and I wanted her approval and for her to always feel a part of my life. Unfortunately, there was never any consistency with what she wanted from me and/or what her expectations would be of me. One day she would be exceptionally supportive of me and the next highly critical of me. She would inform me, through periodic fits of anger, I never, ever did anything for her. I would silently walk away with disbelief to avoid a confrontation. Until one year I'd had enough. I finally replied and listed all the things I had done for her, that made her a part of my life. She became silent and after a long pause under her breath replied *"Oh that's right."* It was an awful feeling to begin rattling off all I'd done for her, and it felt like trying to keep score with someone. I don't like that. Life is too short to keep score. Ours was a complicated relationship.

She wanted and expected perfection of herself and of me, or the illusion of it, presented to the outside world for her own self-worth. Many try to exude that impression. Is it ever achieved? I think not. Oh, but some will present themselves in such a manner so that it is what others immediately think about them and how they want to be perceived. Basically, it becomes boring. We have all been guilty of judging a book by its cover. My goodness ... look at her ... isn't she/he a catch ... physically beautiful people of body and bone structure ... talented ... smart ... they have it all! Or do they? What have they sacrificed? Does anyone go through their entire life being able to say *"I HAD IT ALL?"* After all, we are flawed human beings with countless lessons to be learned, *each and every one of us.* Lessons from our own mistakes, experiences and accomplishments. To be proud, yet humble. Accepting, not shaming. To love and not judge. This journey called life is fascinating, difficult, and ever evolving. Life is hard.

After singing at a women's luncheon one afternoon, I was approached and chatted with a gal who thanked me for coming. She asked about my family, and as per the usual story, I gave her all the pleasing and wonderful news about my children and whatever husband I was married to. She said she wished she could live in my shoes for one day. I got into my car and drove home thinking about her comment and it's never left me. Really? What if I had told her about the daily grind of everyday reality? Well, she would need to choose which day because they certainly were not all roses and sunshine! I can only get through one day at a time. Six children, three marriages and three divorces. Trying to just keep a roof over our heads, food on the table, clothes on our backs and so on. You get the drill. But I could put on my make-up, high heels and a sparkly gown, get on stage and voila, I was coming across as if I had everything. Mother would be proud. ***After all, I am a Miss America*****! HA!**

SISU

"Sisu Dorothy Kathleen. Sisu. Pick yourself up by your bootstraps and keep going. You're stronger than this."

All the time, ALL THE TIME! Mother would repeat this to me. But this I learned was the gift of strength and her setting me up for life. I would need this in my personal and professional life and it has served me well. That doesn't mean there weren't days I didn't want to pick myself up. I wanted to sulk, weep, be left alone for a few hours or maybe a day, or two, or three, because life sure can throw us some curve balls and some are just out of bounds and foul! With some you are taken by surprise and hope that the foul ball doesn't hit someone else in the play. Some are our own choices and others, well yes, are thrown at us. Those are the moments we all have and they are EXHAUSTING!

Sixty-four years later I have begun to understand and realize the depth of how mom was pulling herself up by the bootstraps to face each day with strength and perhaps why she was harder on me than my siblings. She was the epitome of someone exuding an image that was partially false. Mother would have died a million deaths if her circle of friends ever learned of her past.

She had ***SISU!***

She also had a secret.

CHARACTERS

MARY DOROTHY ELEANOR TUOMI

Dorothy Eleanor and her younger brother, Alan, were born in Chicago, Illinois to Finnish immigrants, Eino and Alma Tuomi who each, independently, came to America seeking a better life. Eino found work as a carpenter/contractor and Alma as a housekeeper.

Mother was musical, creative, and a dreamer, and as a very young girl she began following the lives of movie stars, and would emulate the famous women of Hollywood. She once told me her parents thought her behavior strange and they never fully understood her fantasy. She blossomed into a gorgeous woman bestowed with numerous talents. Dorothy Eleanor was bilingual, a veracious reader, gifted in music with a beautiful singing voice, pretty much self-taught piano and accordion, drawing, and writing. She was awarded a scholarship to an art school in Chicago but her parents didn't understand what it was about so it was never pursued. During her high school years, Eino moved the family to Brainerd, Minnesota, where mom and Alan would graduate high school. Alan remained in Brainerd his entire life, loving the solitude of living on the lake. Mom, on the other hand, didn't waste any time leaving after her high school graduation.

She took off for Hollywood, California to become a star. Now, there are two versions to this story. First, as told to me; mom took off with her cousin Beatrice Jarvi and headed west. What Beatrice was going to do out there was never explained. Mom met Archibald Benham while in Hollywood and he proposed on their first date and the court documents have their marriage logged as taking place on November 27, 1944 (while the newspaper announcement has them married on November 23) making her nineteen years of age and him forty-three. Can you even imagine?! Well, perhaps some of you can relate. But what did my grandparents think? Did they approve? He was the same age as them! Did they ever think their daughter would be so impulsive as to take off for Hollywood to become a movie star and end up marrying so quickly?!

The second version was told to my sister, Tody; where after graduation mom was working as a waitress in Brainerd and Archie met her there, convincing her to head west with him. This seems a bit off as I'd like to know what Archie was doing in Brainerd yet he did have a history of traveling from state to state, city to city! Anyway ... that will remain a mystery. According to a newspaper announcement of their marriage Beatrice is named as mom's maid of honor and a fellow named Curley Lockwood served as best man! There's a movie character name for ya! I don't have a clue what Beatrice did after that or where she went. Probably back to Fredrick, South Dakota.

Mom began performing with the USO in Beverly Hills and then auditioned for and was chosen by Sam Goldwyn of Goldwyn Studio/Universal and Warner Bros. to be a *"Goldwyn Girl."* She launched her career as a starlet and began making a name for herself in the movies. One of those movies was called *Night in Paradise*. I've watched it ... believe me ... you are not missing anything! Daddy seemed to have money at the time, and I'm sure he promised her many things ... including the moon or the entire universe. She was his fourth wife but at the time she thought she was only wife number three! After a period of time in California, they moved back to Minnesota. I speculate either he was jealous of the attention toward her or he knew that for many actresses and actors it could mean an unpleasant method of moving up in the Hollywood circles and stardom or did he fear she would learn he was not all he purported to be and run off with someone wealthier and famous.

Upon returning to Minnesota, she became the top model in Minneapolis for Powers and Donaldson's department stores while under contract with

Nilah Brooks Modeling Agency out of Chicago. In 1952 she was crowned the first Mrs. Minnesota and tied for third runner-up at Mrs. America. Her story being she wasn't crowned the winner because the Mrs. America Pageant higher-ups wanted to be paid and whichever husband gave them the most money would solidify their wife would win! Now let's remember this is mom's story as told to me, as told to her by Archie. Archie, we know, was a professional when it came to story fabrication and mother over the years, could and would embellish the truth or make life circumstances fit her reality.

Being that she was beautiful and glamorous, mom looked the part of a wealthy wife in a middle-class neighborhood, and that was an intoxicating image. She maintained that image, though eventually the money ran low and her life became that of a stay-at-home mother of four in a loveless marriage with a difficult if not crazy man. Mother worked hard to keep that pretense by becoming a great bargain shopper and sewing her own clothing. Many hours were passed during the days sitting at the piano and singing. Eventually she joined the local group of women known as "The Armatage Mother Singers" and mom of course, became the soloist. It wasn't long before she started incorporating the local children into her numbers, performing things from *The Sound of Music, The King and I,* and eventually wrote, produced, and directed musicals such as *Snow White,* and *The Wizard of Oz.* They became a yearly tradition and all the Armatage Elementary school children wanted to be a part of them. That alone brought much joy to the kids and their families and probably more fulfillment to mother. I look back and realize the Sisu she had to make something meaningful of her life. Mother was a survivor who knew how to fill her life with what she needed. Soon it would become me. Somehow, she found the money to give me sporadic lessons in piano, dance and later voice. I have a sneaky feeling grandma helped with some of those payments.

She began teaching me songs popularized by movie stars like Jeanette McDonald and Nelson Eddy, Deanna Durbin, and Julie Andrews. She also introduced me to movies with dancers like Leslie Caron, Cyd Charisse, Gene Kelly, Eleanor Powell, Fred Astaire and Ginger Rogers. Our usual weekends consisted of taking the bus to downtown Minneapolis to shop but one Saturday in nineteen sixty-three, instead of shopping, she took me with her to see the first James Bond movie, *Dr. No,* with Sean Connery. She loved the romance in movies and would always sigh when the big kiss finally came between the two main characters. But, when we would watch typical shows on T.V. and people would kiss, her usual comment was *"Ick. Who kisses with their mouth open? That's disgusting and unclean."* I heard that for years. But in my head, I would think *"Well, it sure looks like a lot of people do it!"* It was the beginning of her training me to be 'a good girl.'

ARCHIBALD BENHAM

My dad, as I knew him to be for 64 years, was born in 1901 to Archibald S. Benham and Annie Kelly. (Annie was the daughter of the famous Vaudeville performer John T. Kelly. THAT is another story unto itself!)

He loved and collected beautiful objects and obviously beautiful, talented young women. Marrying four times and producing eight off-spring, supposedly. But who really knows? Archie got around. There could be more! Just sayin'!

1. **Norma Lofgren** ... Married: September 28, 1921 ... April 1922 he was arrested at his father-in-law's home for misconduct ... Divorced 1926, obtained on grounds of cruelty. No children.
2. **Virtue Nicholson** ... Married: October 17, 1932 ... marriage to Arch left her in need of mental health care for a short time. This union produced two sons. Gary and Daryl.
3. **Blondale Marcene (Mickey) McMunn** ... Married: March 25, 1939 ... obtained a divorce on marital affairs. She caught him with the babysitter. This also brought forth two children ... Penelope and Steven.
4. **Dorothy Eleanor Tuomi** ... Married: November 27, 1944 ... remained married until his death but ... thought of divorcing him at one time ... mmm-hmmm! Mother gave birth to four children while married to Archie ...Totiana (Tody), Archibald (Kelley), Dorothy, Sean.

One could describe Archie as charming, debonair, a dapper dresser, a character, con-man, fighter, survivor who was intelligent, quick-witted with exceptionally dry humor. He was intellectually smart and learned how to be street smart. Considering his upbringing I'd say that was a necessity.

By the time Archie was five, he and his two older siblings, John and Jeanette, were placed into the Southern Tier Orphanage Home in upper New York State, Elmire, N.Y. Chemung County. The three siblings lingered there for two years, which was the allowed time frame for children to remain in an orphanage. This was to give parents time to come back and get them if they were on their feet financially. Archibald S. and Annie never visited and did not return to get them so in 1909 they were referred to "The Children's Aid Society" and then placed on the orphan train headed west to Nebraska. Archie was taken in by John Sargeant and his wife Minnie. Yet in a news article it says he was placed with a Fred Young of Plainview, Nebraska. This separated the siblings and one can only imagine the trauma placed upon each of them. First to be abandoned by their parents and now, to lose the last connection of each other.

There are facts documented on Archie's life based on court documents and newspaper clippings and other stories told about him making for great conversation. Archie's military registration papers for WW1 say he was born in 1899 claiming him to be 19 years of age when he was actually 17. His guardian at that time and signature on the papers was that of John Sargent. He tried his hand at numerous careers working at the Nordic Ware Co. in the machine shop, making griddles and then claiming to have invented those griddles. The Rockford, Illinois newspaper ran an advertisement in March of 1926 where he is named as the Beauty Specialist at the "Flower-In-The-Bottle-Beauty-Shoppe." HA! Shall I speculate yet again and say he had convinced someone he was a specialist? That gig didn't last long because soon after he landed in prison! Five months for grand larceny in 1927 in Aberdeen, South Dakota. Then, as he was leaving the prison doors, he was arrested again on the steps of the penitentiary for vehicle theft. Transporting a stolen car. Possibly more, but we may never really know. These newspaper articles show that between marriages, his troubles intensified. A Fremont, Nebraska newspaper article shows he had been accused of rape and/or sexual misconduct with a fourteen-year-old in 1937. Disturbing to learn.

He claimed to have invented the jukebox and pinball machine, and according to sister Pennie and her mom, Mickey, he did design and patent a roulette wheel used in casinos and also designed the "Lulu Punchboard" used in bars. Supposedly he ran off with a carnival at the age of 13 where he ran the Bingo game producing the nick-name "Bingo Benham." According to a photograph book in my possession it looks like he ran and promoted a dance marathon during the 1930's while married to wife number three Mickey McMunn. One dancer named Louis Abbott signed his picture *"To Mrs. Benham the girl I'd like to flirt with."*

Archie owned mineral rights in eight different counties in Montana and luckily, we still have them today. The story isn't clear how he obtained those rights but I once heard he inherited them from his guardian John Sargent. He was a shrewd business man and could have likely bought them himself.

Additionally, he owned a large coin collection that he updated the worth of every year. Mom and he would sit at the dining room table for days, maybe weeks as he read off coin by coin and she typed up all the information for him. It was painstakingly dreadful for her, and she hated it.

Daddy never held a regular nine-to-five job so how we afforded anything was and still remains a mystery to me. Mom would list his occupation on the school forms differently each year ranging from;

1. Benham's Oil Exploration – now, he did have business cards made saying this but it would be an exaggeration.
2. Coin Collector - true.
3. Geologist – he was not. It looked good on paper.

We had a large, round poker table in the basement and I remember evenings daddy would hold poker games with his friends. Men, I didn't know or recognize. One night he won so big the only way the fellow could pay him was with diamond rings. That's how mom obtained her beautiful diamond wedding set. An almost 5 carat solitaire diamond with a band of 3 carat baguette shaped diamonds. You know she loved that!!!!

According to mom, the first word I used in describing daddy was not "dada" but "Gungie." Maybe because he smelled of cigarette smoke. He seemed to live in his bedroom at the end of the hallway playing the card game solitaire on the end of his twin bed while watching the tv show *Gunsmoke*. As I grew up, he gave me the cute nick name "Twinkle Toes" because I was always dancing around the house.

He also had a temper that could be frightening. I saw him once pin my older brother up against the wall by his neck. Scary to witness and left me wondering would he ever do that to me? I recall twice he went after my mother. Both times she quickly grabbed me by the hand and out the door we ran to our neighbors for a few hours. I always wondered why she took me and not any of my other siblings.

Four-year-old Dorothy Kathleen

Dorothy Eleanor

Hollywood Glamour Shot

Dorothy & Archibald Benham

Wedding Photo 1945

Virtue Nichols

Blondale Marcene McMunn (Mickey)

ACT ONE

SCENE 1: EARLY CHILDHOOD

Personally, I felt my childhood was idyllic. But what else did I know? I was the third of four children and my sister, Tody, being eight and a half years older, always seemed like an adult to me. Kelley and I were two-and-a-half years apart with Sean three years behind me. We lived in a wonderful, middle class neighborhood filled with families galore and we never lacked for playmates. It was later in life I realized we probably didn't have the financial means of the other households and in my estimation, we would have been considered low ... very low middle class. We didn't see doctors or dentists on a regular basis, but I thought that was the norm. I recall one required physical and a couple of dental appointments. No Novocain. I didn't know it existed. I sure do now!

I was a very quiet, reserved, and shy little girl with a passion for reading, singing, music and dance, with the performer mentality appearing around the age of two and a half. I'd heard someone on the radio singing the song "He's Got the Whole World in His Hands" and it resonated within me. So, in my little child mind I decided that if I sat on my little step stool directly in front of the air vent alongside of the kitchen counter cabinet, I too would be heard singing on the radio! ME singing "He's Got the Whole World in His Hands."

At around four years of age, I had my first crush! He was tall, slim, fair haired, and blue eyed. He also happened to be our MILKMAN ... George! When I heard his milk truck pulling up or the back-door doorbell ring, I would run to greet him. He exuded an easy-going nature, and I loved how his eyes twinkled when he smiled and spoke to me. Like I was the only person around! I think we had milk delivery for a couple of years but eventually he didn't return, but I remember him to this day! By this time though I had started elementary school and that became the highlight of my days. I attended the afternoon kindergarten class and surprise ... surprise ... music was my favorite part of the day. Mrs. Copeland was a wonderful teacher and taught us many songs to sing and I always eagerly raised my hand to play the lap held autoharp to accompany our songs! I loved school and also loved the library! I read constantly, anxiously waiting for library day each week.

Many a summer month were spent on Gull Lake in Brainerd, Minnesota with my Uncle Alan, Aunt Phyllis and my six cousins. Our days were spent swimming, boating, and skiing at their home on Gull Lake in Brainerd, Minnesota. It was fun and carefree! Uncle Alan would always ask ... *"Where is that, Dorothy Kathleen?"* I'd reply with *"Right here!"* *"Gosh, you are so quiet. Like a little mouse. I thought you'd disappeared."*

Winter months in Minnesota were long and cold but as kids we didn't mind or even really notice as our days were constantly filled with sledding, skating, snowball fights, and sinking up to our hips in snow drifts that seemed six feet high!

I was about six years old when mom tried to introduce me to the world of modeling with Dayton's department store and it was a disaster. I was uncomfortable, eventually began to cry, not wanting to wear the black patent leather Mary-Jane shoes or hold the hand of the little boy in the photo shoot with me! Somehow, they still managed to get a back-to-school ad for the Minneapolis newspaper. A year later we tried it again and success was achieved! I modeled for Dayton's until I was 12 years of age with most of the photo shoots done during the week requiring that I wear pink sponge rollers in my hair during school until mom came to get me, and we then rode the city bus to downtown Minneapolis. Sometimes after a modeling shoot mom would take me for lunch in the basement of Powers Department store to the cafeteria and I would have French Fries and a coke! Still my favorite but now add a grilled cheese and I am very happy! Other days mom and I went to the Elks Club in downtown Minneapolis where daddy was a member. Walking through the door you immediately entered into a small, dimly lit room giving the impression of something special and fancy if not a bit mysterious. We would sit at the bar and mom would order me the "Shirley Temple" made of ginger ale with a splash of grenadine topped off with a cherry! What did mom order? Well, she probably had a stiff drink! HA! That's a total guess on my part! Maybe a *really good* guess! Then we would take the bus home.

Throughout my elementary years, I usually walked to and from school with friends or my brothers. The days I walked alone mother would warn me to never accept a ride from anyone and do not get in a stranger's car even if they offered me candy or wanted me to go see their new puppy or kitten. I will say she was right. There were two times during my elementary years that I was approached. The first time I might have been walking home after a piano lesson and one block away a man pulled his car over to the side of the street I was walking on (the wrong side for him) and asked if I wanted candy. Here it was. The moment mother had warned me about. I said nothing to him but turned and looked straight ahead picking up my pace and trying to appear unruffled as I walked the last block home. Let's just say he didn't have a genuine smile or twinkly blue eyes like George the milk man or my Uncle Alan. I was glad to be in the safety of my home. The second time happened a couple of years later, I guess I was about sixth grade. Mother needed a sympathy card and asked me to walk the few blocks to the local corner store and pick one up. Nothing floral or too decorated. Something simple and clean. Gold, silver or black lettering would be just fine. I found one in gold lettering with a simple greeting of condolences and began my walk home. I decided to stay on the busier street of Penn Avenue rather than the shortcut through the neighborhood when a car full of teenage boys pulled over to the curb whistling and calling me names ... cat calling was the term I learned later in life. *"Come on in sweety, you look so nice, we will give you a ride where ever you want to go or need to get to. Come on get in cutie."* Again, I said nothing but looked straight ahead and made it home without incident.

Friday and Saturday nights were my favorites because we were allowed to stay up late watching *Tarzan* with Johnny Weissmuller, Abbott and Costello or horror movies like *Dracula*, *The Werewolf*, *The Mummy* until midnight when the television stations played the National Anthem and turned off until morning. Sunday nights we always watched *The Ed Sullivan Show* and every September along with the rest of America, we made popcorn and watched *The Miss America Pageant* immediately prompting grandma to have me practice walking with a book on my head to learn how to walk "queenly", with a smooth gait, and my younger brother Sean would then start his chicken walk dance with a book on his head making us roar with laughter! I don't recall the exact year but think it may have been around fifth grade when Grandma said to me in her Finnish accent, *"Dooroty Gasoleene, you work hard, be goot gurl and someday you be Miss America too."* Little did we know. Perhaps she knew.

By sixth grade white Go-Go boots were all the rage and mom found a pair for me! Intro fashion into my life via Mom and Tody. They decided I should cut bangs just like the model on one of the fashion magazines with Tody as the beautician. She proceeded to cut the front portion of my waist length hair level to my chin. Let's just say it wasn't the most attractive look but all that could be done now was let them grow out. That same weekend they thought it would be fun to pierce my ears, and I was game because as a ten-year-old I felt they were practically professionals and knew everything about fashion! This would be fantastic because not many girls my age had pierced ears. I sat on the bathroom counter as Tody proceeded to freeze my ear lobes with ice and then came the needle! A sewing needle being manipulated back and forth, back and forth being captured by a potato on the other side until she felt the hole was large enough to put in the tiny gold earrings. To top it off, mom was now nervous about my teacher noticing I had pierced ears and decided it would be best for me to wear my hair in pigtails. Pigtails with chin length bangs and let's say again ... was not the best look. So, I attend school and every day all the while nervous thinking my teacher will find out and what would I say. That's exactly what happened! It took about a week and a half of my hair styled in the same pigtails with weird bangs until my teacher eventually became suspicious and asked if I had pierced ears. Our secret was discovered, and I was put on the spot. All I could muster out was *"Yes."* What a relief for me when she commented that they looked very cute! I told mom immediately after school and I didn't have to wear pigtails again! Thank goodness.

SCENE 2: JR. HIGH

It was pretty exciting to begin middle school at Susan B. Anthony Jr. High knowing there would be many other students from surrounding neighborhoods filling the large hallways to capacity. Even if I did start the year on crutches with a banged-up leg from falling off my bike the day before classes began. Dress codes were implemented so girls had to wear skirts or dresses, no slacks and definitely no jeans for the boys. Mom said I could start shaving my legs but only up to the knee cap. That seemed odd because skirts and dresses were short and there was hair on my thighs too so why not shave the entire leg? I decided it was mom needing control. That lasted about two weeks and I just went ahead and shaved the entire leg. She never noticed. Mrs. Olson was my homeroom teacher all three years at Anthony Jr. High. Her salt and pepper hair always done perfectly into a high, full updo that swept across her forehead resembling the "Gibson Girl". She was a kind lady with a gentle demeanor and took a liking to me, asking for my help with different tasks during homeroom time and every so often with after school projects and then she would drive me home. I liked that I could be of help and that an adult would think me capable of assisting. I felt important. I was always in a choir, which I loved and in gym classes we were introduced to gymnastics! Now THIS was FUN! The pommel horse, uneven bars, parallel bars, balance beam, and trampoline. I even liked the high jump and the long jump. These were areas I felt my competitive nature rise.

The summer between seventh and eighth grade the hideous chin length bangs had pretty much grown out but now mother decided my hair was getting too dark so she bought a box of blonde hair coloring. She applied it believing my hair would end up the same color blonde as the model pictured on the cover. Oh boy ... my hair did not react well and turned an orangish-strawberry blonde and now she didn't want me to tell anyone she lightened it in hopes people would just think it had been "sun-kissed" as we used to say. Notice? Everyone noticed and one of the older girls in the neighborhood had a boyfriend who nick-named me "two-tone!" Hair options were not discussed again until my college days.

With Tody off at college many evenings were spent with mother sitting on my bed, as we listened to different opera singers, we discussed their technique and interpretation of each aria before I would drift off to sleep.

My favorite soprano being Anna Moffo and of course Joan Sutherland was grand and the occasional recording of Maria Callas, Beverly Sills, Claudia Muzio, Marion Anderson, Lily Pons and others. But it was Moffo I seemed to identify with the most. Both she and Sutherland had impeccable pitch and clarity. This was my introduction to the classics and inception of my love of opera.

Mom started me on voice lessons with a former teacher of Tody's who was a lovely woman but almost two years later I told mom I wasn't grasping what she wanted me to do with the support and breathing and it felt backward from what she and Tody ever spoke about. I wasn't sure if it was me unable to understand the complexity of singing or if this was a new way of teaching support and breath control. I'd watched Tody sing and mother sing with them showing me very early on what "support" entailed. Would a different teacher make a difference? Immediately mom set out to find another voice teacher and before the end of ninth grade she found Adyline Felsted. This, THIS woman was the right teacher for me. I was now fourteen and finishing ninth grade. Everything Adyline said and taught me I comprehended immediately. The intricate balance of breathing, support, tonal placement, and diction fell into place! I looked up to this petite woman with a personality larger than life, so direct, no nonsense, funny, always running late, baking until the wee hours of the morning, delivering Meals on Wheels to those in need, and saving animals! She was an Energizer Bunny! Adyline could make anyone feel they were capable of achieving any goal. Her presence in my life was one of the greatest blessings bestowed upon me and will always remain a monumental impact on my life. She was my mentor and friend.

Tody became engaged and married the summer before I entered ninth grade and I was one of her bridesmaids! Not a Junior Bridesmaid but a BRIDESMAID! The morning of the wedding mom sent me and my cousin Roxanne to the local hair salon to have our hair professionally done in updo's. THIS was exciting and such a treat! WELL ... upon completion my waist length hair looked like two bee hives one atop the other! It was awful! Roxanne and I walked home, me trying to balance the monstrosity upon my head, and as we entered through the front door, everyone gasped in horror at my hairdo. It felt as if we removed 500 bobby pins and still unable to get a brush through the hairspray, we all agreed it would be best for me to jump in the shower, wash out the spray and wear it down in a more fitting hairstyle for a 13-year-old. We wore beautiful powder blue chiffon dresses that felt elegant and made me feel like a grown up!

As a ninth grader I joined the gymnastics competitive team in floor exercise and in the few competitions we participated in, I always took second place due to the fact that I could dance and do a few easy tumbling stunts but nothing exceptional. I was in awe of those girls that were capable of much more difficult tumbling. It simply was great fun being part of this team!

This choir year brought me my first solo, "O Holy Night." This was exciting and nerve-wracking at the same time! During the Christmas season school choirs were given the opportunity to perform at Southdale Shopping Center (the first indoor shopping mall in the country) in the center courtyard. Our choir was scheduled for one of the performance slots and we would be singing "O Holy Night." As I stepped forward to sing my legs began shaking and I'm sure my voice was trembling. I got through it but was mortified that I couldn't control the nerves. I vowed that night being nervous wouldn't suffice, and not only did I need to enjoy the moment, it needed to be pleasant for the audience. The second half of ninth grade, a student teacher arrived and was allowed to place us in the vocal section she felt best. Surprisingly, she put me in as an alto, when I always thought I was definitely a soprano as did mom and my private teacher, but I remained in the alto section and in retrospect I appreciate that half of the year because I learned harmony. Our musical production that year was *Calamity Jane*. I was not selected for the role of Calamity, but given the role of Susan Miller. A young woman who falls in love with a song and dance man named, Francis Fryer. He and I had one song and dance routine together and opening night it was me who turned the wrong way during our number and our backsides collided! I'm sure a look of horror was on my face, but somehow it translated into something humorous and was kept in the remaining performances.

My final year in junior high would soon be over with new and exciting challenges to look forward to entering senior high. The choral directors from the two neighboring high schools, Washburn High and Southwest High, always came at the end of the ninth-grade year to test and audition those of us desiring to sing in their choirs come tenth grade. They were both considered quality choral directors, but Mr. Dahle was always considered the best, or so I heard. I would sing for Mr. O.B. Dahle from Southwest and knew that he was an important man in the Minnesota music school systems. Tody had been a soloist in his choir and brother Kelley had him for a study hall. Everyone wanted to be in his choir and us girls knew we were really auditioning for the Sophomore girls' choir the "Choralettes" because junior and senior students filled the soprano or alto openings in the main choir. The day approached and Mr. Dahle would call our names according to sections. He tested our pitch, memory, and vocal range. Before long I heard my name called and stepped forward to begin my testing. He paused half way through and asked, *"Why are you in the alto section?"* And my response was *"That's where I was placed!"* His response *"You are a soprano!"* A soprano I was! A few weeks passed and then the list of those who made the choirs was sent and posted. Most of us made the "Choralettes" and high school was looking like more fun each day!

With choir auditions done my next goal was to try out for the high school dance line called the "Southwest Indianettes." Sister Tody had been an Indianette and captain her senior year. A few times they practiced in our back yard and I was mesmerized watching them dance. The try-outs were held at the end of ninth grade because practices would be all summer before school began in the fall. My childhood friend Joelle was two years older than me and on the dance line. She and I took dance class together growing up, and she thought I would make the "A" squad team. Coming from her it was a great boost to my self-confidence. Realistically most girls made the "B" squad their first year and then would have a better chance of making the A squad by 11th grade. Either way, I just wanted to dance! That evening, after auditions, I was in the living room showing mother what had been expected of us and right then and there, out the side corner window a group of girls dressed in purple and white came running toward the house! I froze and said, *"Mom...oh my gosh! I must have made the squad ... I mean the A squad ... here they come! Mom, look out the window!"* and by then they were at my door cheering and taking me with them. I received my necklace of a silver Indian tom-tom! I did it! I made the A squad as a tenth grader! As it turned out, I was one of four sophomores that year to make the "A" squad. The summer was filled with daily dance line practices, babysitting, and voice lessons with Adyline. Life was exciting for this 14-year-old rising sophomore!

SCENE 3: HIGH SCHOOL

Entering the majestic front doors of the high school was exhilarating and the first thing I noticed on the floor was the most beautiful inlaid stone medallion of an Indian Chief! Our school mascot! I was so proud to be a Southwest Indian and the year was off to a wonderful start with choir and solo opportunities making me feel like a real singer. District and State vocal ratings were starting to take place and would continue over the next three years. I was proud, but really more relieved, to always be rated in the "superior" category. We had daily dance-line practices and performances during pep-fests, the halftimes for Football and Basketball games or helping cheer on our Hockey teams. On game days we wore our Tom-Tom necklace and purple jumpers to school to show support and school spirit! It gave me an immediate feeling of belonging.

The very first week of school my homeroom teacher appointed me the student council representative for our class. Yikes! Not something I was looking to be part of but do you say no to being appointed? I think not! Did he sense leadership qualities in me or observe my reserved, shy nature and thought it might help me come out of my shell? This position required members at every meeting and then reporting back to your homeroom class what had been discussed. It was uncomfortable for me to get up and speak in front of others but turned out to be a great teaching tool with immeasurable impact on my confidence and ability to present myself in front of my peers and years later a benefit for interviewing.

The summer months were now filled with Indianette practices, babysitting, voice lessons, and the occasional passing of time at the Southdale Shopping Mall with a friend. One particular afternoon as we rode the escalator in Dayton's Department store up to the girls' clothing department, a man directly behind us began asking me questions ... *"Excuse me ... are you a native Minnesotan? How old are you? What nationality are you?"* etc. He then asked if he could take photos of me tomorrow for a story he was doing about the mid-west and its Scandinavian heritage. I told him I would need to speak with my parents about it, so he gave me his card ... the name? ... Ron Galella.

FYI:

[1]*Ronald Edward Galella is an American photographer, known as a pioneer paparazzo. Dubbed "Paparazzo Extraordinaire" by Newsweek and "the Godfather of the U.S. paparazzi culture" by Time magazine and Vanity Fair, he is regarded by Harper's Bazaar as "arguably the most controversial paparazzo of all time". He immortalized many celebrities out of the public eye and gained notice for his feuds with some of them, including Jacqueline Onassis and Marlon Brando Despite the numerous controversies, Galella's work has been praised and exhibited in art galleries worldwide and he was cited by Andy Warhol as his favorite photographer.*

Upon returning home after my shopping excursion, I gave the card to mother with her response being, she would think about it and let me know. A couple hours later she said she would allow the photo session. Reflecting on this memory I realize mother might have never discussed it with daddy but instead called O.B. Dahle for his opinion because, and low and behold ... wait for it ... he drove us out there the following day. Ron Galella took a few photos of me in my bathing suit by the hotel pool. I remember it being an overcast day, not particularly warm and only taking about an hour. I hadn't a clue who he was, but mother more than likely did and now I wonder if secretly, mother hoped he would photograph her as well. Given her history in the movie and modeling world of bye-gone days. She was all dolled up! Funny how at the time I didn't find it all that strange Mr. Dahle would drive us. I trusted the adults in my life and looked at him as a mentor. I now question why she would have involved Mr. Dahle ... hmmmm. Because mother didn't drive, she was brilliant at knowing how to use the bus system so why Mr. Dahle? Did she not want daddy involved, maybe daddy refused to drive, maybe daddy was out of town and I don't remember ... or just a great excuse to see Mr. Dahle. Did she know Mr. Dahle better than anyone could or would suspect? After all, he did offer me rides home on those late rehearsal days. *Hmmmmmmm ...*

Adyline had me preparing for vocal scholarship competitions that would take place over the next couple of years such as The Thursday Musical Club, Tuesday Musical Club and Mr. Dahle had me compete for the Evergreen Scholarship Award. All of which I took first place in and the money helped pay for my vocal lessons. Once school started the only change my junior year brought was singing in the large Main School Choir while the usual

---

[1] Background information obtained from Wikipedia

dance-line practices, church choir, performances, and voice lessons continued. When spring arrived, Mr. Dahle had my friend Dan McMullin and me audition for the opportunity to take part in the *American Youth Performs Choir*. Dan and I were accepted, and we were the only two soloists chosen from Minnesota that year! It meant flying out to Washington D.C. and staying with host families. Since this was my first time on an airplane it was a big deal! There would be a choir and orchestra consisting of high school students from all over the country. The concert was held at the *John F. Kennedy Performing Arts Center* with us performing Leonard Bernstein's "Chichester Psalms" with him conducting! What an experience! Little did I know that many years later I would sing for him again ... his composition ... but this time as a soloist!

Being a senior in high school naturally held more excitement. The year began with my being crowned Homecoming Queen and I was honored. It really doesn't get much better than that. When you realize your peers like you and think highly enough of you to be their representative.

Eve Schwartz and I had been voted co-captains of the dance-line bringing another level of responsibility. We would take turns watching the dance routines making corrections and suggestions. There came a day that I began to question my leadership abilities. It was my turn to observe a final run-through for the afternoon and when they finished, I blew my top! *"Really? You think this will suffice? Well, it won't. So, get your kicks up, energy up, point your toes, and show some interest in what we do. I am not going out there to perform if we aren't all invested! We are a group and need to work like a team with consistency!"* Silence. They were so quiet. I made them run through it again ... it was better. As I drove home, I replayed this over and over again in my head wondering *who am I?* Where did that come from? Why did I blow, yell and become angry with them? Is this who I am? Was I tired or stressed? They probably all hate me now. Yet, somehow, at that moment, I didn't mind if they liked me or not. I was part of a team ... this team ... and I wanted us to be the best we could be. Perfectionism. I was beginning to expect it of myself, but did I have the right to expect it of others?

November came quickly and daddy had a heart attack. He spent a few days at Southdale Fairview Hospital before being taken to the Veterans Hospital in Minneapolis where to say he was a handful, was an understatement. Back in that day smoking was allowed in hospital rooms and he eventually set his room on fire. They banned him from smoking causing him to get angry. OF COURSE, he's going to get angry! He smoked the majority of his life! Who knows, maybe he was ten when he started that habit and was now going through nicotine withdrawal. He began physically attacking the nurses resulting with his arms being put in restraints tied to the bed rails. It was unsettling to witness your parent being treated in such a manner yet knowing the hospital staff's safety came first.

The few times my brother Sean and I would visit Daddy, he tried convincing us to buy him cigarettes. He suggested we should hide them in the ceiling fixture where they wouldn't be detected. He also wanted us to release his wrists from the bed rails! That was our cue to exit.

The first week of December he was transferred to the Veterans Hospital in St. Cloud, Minnesota where he would remain and have twenty-four-hour care but three days after being transferred daddy had a stroke and died. His burial was scheduled for December eleventh, my seventeenth birthday, and since daddy was an atheist, there would not be a church service. Only a graveside service out in the cold with lots of snow on the ground, a minister reading and saying a few things, and a few of my girlfriends who came to be with me, which was very nice.

I felt little emotion just wanting to get out of the cold and back home. To this day I'm not sure if that was some survival mechanism or because I never felt close to him. Heck, I barely knew when he was home or not. Mother started working at JC Penney in the drapery department to make ends meet. Make ends meet? That may be the wrong terminology because I don't know how we had money or how the bills were paid when daddy was alive. I had no idea where any money was, or would have been coming from, as daddy didn't work; so what payments would mother be receiving? Death benefits? Social Security?

Because Tody and her husband Bob were living out of state, and Kelley in the Navy, it left my younger brother Sean and me at home with my being the only driver. Mother had never driven and personally I felt she loved being chauffeured around. If she wasn't able to take the bus, I would drive her to and from work. But hey ... the evenings I didn't pick her up, when I would be at a school game dancing or cheering in the stands ... maybe someone else picked her up. Maybe she didn't take the bus home! Just speculating ... *hmmmm* ... *hmmmm* .....

Daddy is gone, mom is working, life has changed slightly but I'm involved with enough school activities to keep me very busy, and moving forward. Christmas was around the corner and that year the fashion rage was decoupaged handbags. They could be pricey if purchased in a store so many people were trying their own hand at making them or basically decoupaging anything to give as Christmas gifts. Mother decided we should try our hand at some form of it. OK! That would be a fun and artistic challenge! She decided I should decoupage a trash can with sheet music for Mr. Dahle and give it to him as a Christmas gift, and as a thank you for being such a great teacher.

Initially, my silent gut response was ... why? And why a trash can? She more than likely had an old trash can in the house and thought we could spruce it up with the decoupage. Personally, I felt it was a strange idea, as I had never given a teacher a gift before, but I said nothing and proceeded to apply the sheet music on to the trash can, finishing it with the glaze of the decoupage. I only wish I could remember what song was printed on the sheet music. That could have been very telling and given great insight to a developing relationship. She then instructed me to write him a note, dictating the entire message while referring to him as "Maestro Dahle" ... um ... ok ... that too was dramatic. I don't speak like that and had never referred to him as maestro. She then told me to immediately drive the gift over to his home and present it to him that night. That felt REALLY weird to me but again did as she instructed. Off I drove to deliver the homemade gift. Mr. Dahle appeared at his front door, I handed the gift to him and said Merry Christmas. He seemed pleased and thanked me as I turned to leave. It all seemed off to me.

A few months later I picked up on the fact that they might be interested in one another the night Mr. Dahle drove me home after a concert. He walked me to the front door and through the three little door windows I saw mother in a lovely nightgown and robe. Similar to the sexy peignoir sets women wore in the movies! Where the hell did she get this nightgown? She never owned or wore those slinky nighties. There she was stretched out on the sofa in a seductive pose with one arm placed above her head and the other draped alongside her body. Trying to act nonchalantly and only slightly surprised when she heard me knock, she then devilishly rose from the sofa and elegantly, as if floating on air, strode to the door with one arm reaching toward us and all I can think, as I observe this, is 'what is she doing?' The door opened with her smiling, practically batting her lashes, no ... she WAS batting her eyelashes and her body language said much more! She opened the door and said, in a breathy, sweet as pie voice, *"Oh my. I must have fallen asleep!"*

As she smoothed the peignoir gown along her body, like it had become twisted. IT had not. WOW! Just wow! I greeted her with *"Hi mom"*, entered quickly, thanked Mr. Dahle and retreated to my room. Who knows what happened after that! I ignored it and decided to not give it another thought. Ignoring it didn't work very well because not long after the entire school was buzzing with the news, they were an item.

She was looked upon by some people as *"the other woman"* because Mr. Dahle was a married man, though none of us had ever seen or heard of her, and he decided to leave his wife for my mother. But neither of them gave it another thought because they were happy. All in all, as I now speculate, they may have been interacting with one another far longer than I or anyone else realized. DO YA THINK?! Mom, mom, mom ... things are becoming clearer each day.

For a few months, in my senior year I dated my friend Craig until mom practically accused me of being a hussy with him. Here's the story; Craig and I were doing some work for Mr. Dahle in his office, which was attached directly to the choir room where he was working with other classmates; the door was open but when he came through the door Craig happened to place his hand on my leg ... just above my knee to be exact, and Mr. Dahle called and told my mother. Well, when I got home that evening, she dove into me with a fury of anger accusing me of letting him touch me, how wrong that was, and I would be considered loose. Good God! The most we ever did was kiss! The dating ended, but we remained friends for life. He even remained friends with mother and Mr. Dahle. Can you say confusing? I should add that Craig was a fine musician with aspirations of being a concert pianist. His dream easily in his grasp until he was diagnosed with MLS. He passed away in 2017. Gone too soon. I miss his contagious laughter, wit, intelligence, smile and friendship.

I'm not sure when O.B. (as we now refer to him) started divorce proceedings from his wife but all of a sudden, he is in an apartment, our home is up for sale, mom and O.B. have purchased a new home closer to the high school and near Lake Calhoun. A lovely area. While all of this is transpiring, my reaction was to remain focused, keep moving forward with my vocal training, and finishing my last year of high school.

I'm pretty sure it was soon after graduation when mother and I got into an argument. It must have been an insignificant reason for I don't remember what it was about, only her reaction and that O.B. was standing there listening and watching. More than likely, I wanted to go somewhere or do something she didn't agree with or trust. She told me no and when I asked why or just tried to explain what I wanted to do, she flew into a rage screaming at me and to not disagree with her. I can still picture O.B. standing in the living room saying nothing, probably in shock witnessing what was unfolding, mother at the base of the stairs and me halfway up the staircase. I was so tired of not being trusted. I was a good girl. Not a foolish girl. It ended with me screaming back telling her I was tired of her overbearing treatment and distrust toward me. I had never been allowed to go to any party gatherings because she worried too much. I'm pretty sure I ended it with something to the effect of *"I don't even like you, YOU....YOU WOMAN!"* That to me was like a cuss word because I refused to call her mom. I have an occasional hearty laugh over that memory even today! It ended up with O.B. taking me out of the house and we went for a car ride to talk and let me calm down. But when we returned, she didn't want me in the house so she flew me to Tody and Bob's home in Illinois for a week. I guess so she could gather herself. I was miserable.

I returned home soon enough to attend the University of Minnesota summer music camp with a few other friends from high school and though I wasn't ecstatic about attending, I knew it would probably be a good experience that would push me further out of my introverted comfort zone.

I would meet other musicians from around the Twin Cities and Minnesota. We stayed on campus in the dorms, having roommates, going to classes such as theory, voice lessons, production, and performance structure felt like a glimpse into college life. My high school friend Barb and I were given the same voice teacher with scheduled lessons back-to-back, so we went together and listened to each other's lessons. They took place in the gymnasium where the piano was placed at one end of the room. My lesson was on the schedule first, so the teacher started the vocalizing scales and warm up.

Everything seemed fine until the last vocal exercise when she instructed me to scream at the clock on the wall at the other end of the gym. I quickly glanced over at Barb who also seemed a bit shocked by this request. I looked back at the teacher and questioned this tactic asking her if she really wanted a scream or some other vocal sound. Should it be an actual musical sound that we try to produce with as much volume as possible? No... she wanted me to scream at the clock. My first thought was how bizarre and absolutely crazy. Why would any instructor have any singer do this? I already had five years of vocal training and three years of those years with Adyline. I was certain she wouldn't agree with this so-called technique. I obliged the teacher and after doing it to her liking she had me sing some repertoire.

I was no longer inspired to sing but Barb and I both did as instructed ending up with barely a speaking voice. I decided to call O.B. and mom and explain what was happening telling them I wouldn't go back and take another lesson. At the fresh young age of seventeen I was labeled "Diva." HA! So be it ... I was okay with that. I don't recall if Barb continued with lessons.

A second incident happened about a week into camp when one of the music theory class teachers approached me and asked if I would come to his apartment and listen to music with him. What? How weird I thought. This definitely didn't feel right. My stomach felt nervous with him approaching me this way. My gut told me to run. Why me? Ick ... I wasn't about to do that. In my ear, I could hear mom's warning about not talking to or accepting rides with strangers and to leave if something felt wrong. It was the same feeling I had as a child when approached by strangers in their cars and it would not be the last. I told him no and once again phoned mom and O.B. told them the circumstances and obviously he was reported because after that, every time he saw me in the hallways he would stop and stare at me. Glare at me and obviously try to make me feel uncomfortable. Which of course it did. He was successful in doing that. My little Diva self-reported yet another teacher. I was retreating back into the safety of my shell wanting to leave and be in the safety of my home, at the lake with cousins, babysitting, anything but there on that campus. I stayed because it cost my mom and O.B. money for me to attend but relief washed over me when camp came to an end. Sadly, it was a camp I could have done without and wish I would have come away with something positive other than appearing as someone who complained.

SCENE 4: COLLEGE

For the third time in my life, I took a seat on an airplane and this time headed to North Carolina School of the Arts in Winston-Salem. The flight seemed long, and the layover was hours! After landing I grabbed a taxi and made it in time for registration. Going from table to table signing up for class schedules and dorm room assignments. The woman handed me my class schedule and said, "I have a feeling your nick name will be Sunshine!"

How sweet was that? I'll take it! At first, I was so excited to begin my studies but it soon faded. Freshman were not allowed to perform — that was frustrating. We took language classes, voice lessons, theory, dance/movement, piano, and required to be in the choir, but even that was dull. The choral director was nothing close to what I experienced in high school singing under the direction of O.B. Dahle. It was boring, the music was boring and maybe I was unable to bend and accept anything different. My voice teacher was nice, but he didn't hold a candle to Adyline and left me feeling unchallenged. I'd lost interest. The few memories of this school year that impacted me were when I was sitting outside the dance class rooms, watching the dancers and wishing I was one of them. Such a disciplined, beautiful sight. I attended all of the dance productions soon realizing this was much more a dance school than vocal school.

Unexpectedly, Grandma Alma died during this year and I felt that loss deeply but grateful she died peacefully in her sleep. I cherish the memories of her twinkling eyes, cute Finnish accent, laughter, and her red apple cheeks! Then one day at lunch, as I sat alone, the violin teacher came and took a seat at my table wanting to ask me a few questions. He told me the other students didn't think I spoke English being as I was from Minnesota and Scandinavian in my appearance, so he came to find out.

Finlander's aren't really considered Scandinavian. Geographically Finland doesn't share the Scandinavian peninsula. Finland is considered a Nordic country like Iceland. The Finns are Finno-Ugric people. Whatever the heck that really means. Their language is related to Estonian and Hungarian. There, that's a little history lesson! I was told my genetic make-up was Finnish, Russian, English, Irish, and Scottish. Anyway, he asked me to pronounce certain words that he thought I would pronounce like a Canadian. How silly I thought. I had spoken to numerous students in my classes and one fellow classmate asked me if we had polar bears in Minnesota because it was so far north ... on the Canadian border. GEESH! Really?

The most impactful memory was during the first semester when my fellow classmate, a boy in my theory class who was a percussion major and appeared very smart, kind of quiet as well, asked if I wanted to get together and discuss the class homework and listen to what was assigned and required of us. We were sitting in his dorm room talking about class and of course music when, out of the blue, he asked me to be his girlfriend. What? WOW ... We barely knew one another. This was the first time outside of class we had gotten together as friends. Never held hands. Never a kiss. We were classmates, basically strangers. I looked at him and said *"No."* Prompting his next question, *"Why, because I'm black?"* WHOA ... that set me back for a second and when I composed myself told him, *"No, we are classmates and friends and how was I to feel romantic about him or agree to be his girlfriend when we knew nothing about one another?"*

This has bothered me ever since. Why would he ask such a thing? Because he felt slighted? No one had ever asked me anything of the sort. My goodness, I realized I never looked at the color of people's skin. One of my dearest friends in high school was a black boy named Dorian, a gifted singer and we hung out all the time. Why? Why would someone ask such a thing? I had turned down a romantic relationship, and he thought it was because of his color? Never had I experienced, been confronted, or questioned so boldly as to the color of one's skin. This was foreign to me. It lost me his friendship. As the year progressed North Carolina School of the Arts didn't feel like the right college and partly because I was bored. So, I left after the first year.

This prompted O.B. to make some phone calls in search of a voice teacher. He was directed to someone that was considered one of the best in the country at Lawrence University's Music Conservatory in Appleton, Wisconsin. By summer I was enrolled for the fall semester and once again, not even a full semester into the school year, I found her technique of vocal singing a nightmare. She taught a method of training that caused me to lose my entire middle range. The method was to push the lower voice into the upper instead of the blending technique of Adyline. I questioned myself and my own intellect. What is it that I am not understanding? Is it *ME*?

At Thanksgiving I was home and tried singing for my parents in the technique that Adyline taught and they were mortified. I went to Adyline, and she turned white as a ghost saying *"I thought that technique went out with the dark ages!"*

I had some lower notes and most of my upper but the middle range was gone unless I forced the sound. THAT was frightening to me ... how quickly something new can destroy years of work. I went back to finish the semester knowing I would not return to Lawrence after Christmas. I went to my lessons but when I practiced, I did what Adyline had taught me and started the process of rebuilding my voice! The new plan was to return to Minnesota and study with Adyline at one of the colleges where she taught. In hindsight, it's probably what should have been considered first and foremost. Why stray from a teacher and method that worked? I would have been glad to have stayed in Minnesota and attend college, but in mom and O.B.'s minds I'm sure they thought I should move on to experience something new.

Over the Christmas break, I gently vocalized two to three times a day regaining my vocal blend and middle range strength. I visited all the colleges at which Adyline taught, and after meeting with Dr. Dale Warland, who was not only the founder of the well-known Dale Warland Singers but also the choral director at Macalester College in St. Paul, Minnesota, I decided that's where I belonged. Spring semester began and it felt like the perfect fit for me. Dr. Warland was a master of choral directing, and singing under his direction as a member of the Macalester choir and as a soloist introduced me to more diverse music and choral technique. Dr. Edward Forner, director of the Orchestra Department, was my appointed counselor and had me tour with the orchestra as soloist. So, here I was touring with both the choir and orchestra and finally felt I was growing as a musician and person. Dale Warland recalled later in a newspaper interview, how ill I would become with motion sickness while riding on the tour buses, and amazed at how I could get off the bus, quickly change into our choir dress for a concert, and still sing well! All in all, everything felt right. I'd found my college. Hmmmm ... reminds me of *The Wizard of Oz* when Glinda tells Dorothy she didn't need to look further than her own backyard.

Adyline had me participate in the Schubert Club Vocal competition that spring. My friend Dan McMullin from high school days did too! I did not win but came in second place with a small scholarship award. I knew Adyline would have me try again the next year and as usual I studied with her throughout the summer looking forward to the start of school in the fall!

This was the summer I was made aware that other people did not think Tody and I were sisters. These comments, of course did not come from those people we grew up with, but those individuals meeting us or me for the first time. The remarks became *"You're Tody's sister? You don't look anything alike!"* We would laugh and shrug it off because of course we were sisters! She looked more like mom with daddy's coloring and I had daddy's longer face and moms fairer coloring. This would continue on for many decades.

Mother and Me

Grandma Alma and Me

Totiana, Mom, Kelley, Me, Sean

Dayton's Modeling Ad

My Sixth Grade School Photo

Photo of Me by Ron Galella

THESE ST. PAUL and Minneapolis high school students will be among 110 instrumentalists and 120 vocalists chosen from throughout all 50 states who will perform May 9 in the John F. Kennedy Performing Arts Center in Washington, D.C. They will leave this coming week to take part in the program sponsored by American Youth Performs, Inc. Their selection is considered an honor, since each state is limited to a very few. These are the only performers from Minnesota. Some of the large states have even fewer representatives. The students are, back row, from left, Cara Mia Antonello, Mounds View High, and Scott Adelman, Norman Bolter and Victor Constanzi, all of Highland Park High. In front, from Minneapolis, are Dan McMullin, and Dorothy Benham, both from Southwest High.

News Story Featuring American Youth
Performance in Washington, DC

Homecoming Photo

High School Graduation Photo

Macalester College Choir

Directed by Dale Warland

ACT TWO

SCENE 1: THE JOURNEY BEGINS

Fall of 1975 resumed at Macalester College with classes in full swing and also, as was tradition, time to watch *The Miss America Pageant.* Mom and O.B. were at Martha and Walley Hawkins' home watching while my friend Julie and I watched at my house. Tawney Godin a striking, statuesque brunette who played a lovely piano composition of her own was crowned Miss America 1976 and that was the year it really dawned on me this was an educational scholarship program and I could possibly win some money for school or lessons! That night I decided to compete. Especially since I had already won the vocal scholarship competitions for my grade and age category. I turned to Julie and said, *"I think I should give this Miss America Pageant a whirl and try to win some money for school and voice lessons."* When mom and O.B. got home that evening I told them that I was ready to compete and by Monday, O.B. found an open pageant – Miss South St. Paul! Open meaning it would allow an outsider to compete. Ideally cities or towns preferred if you were a resident.

63

All of the Minneapolis pageants had already taken place, and this was my one opportunity. Miss South St. Paul was scheduled for October 25th at the South St. Paul High School. Having little over a month to prepare, mom and I went to work deciding what I should sing. An opera aria in Italian, French or German. Perhaps an Art song? What would the judges want to hear?

I knew nothing about this pageant program. A week later on Sunday night I watched a PBS special featuring Metropolitan opera singer, Roberta Peters singing "Adele's Laughing Song" from *Die Fledermaus*. That's IT! That was my song. It showed range, personality and humor! Mom went downtown to purchase the sheet music only to find the words differed from those Roberta sang. Her next stop was the Minneapolis library where in the archived music section she found the no longer published sheet music and words. Back then they allowed her to make a copy, and we were off to the races!

Over the next four weeks, Adyline worked with me on the vocal interpretation and I basically copied Roberta's physical interpretation. Next I needed a one-piece swimsuit. Where? WHERE in Minnesota do you find a swimsuit when it's no longer swimsuit weather? The Curtis Hotel in downtown Minneapolis Resort Shop, that's where, and even better is when it's on sale for $12.00 in white. Done! Now I would need an interview dress. We found a cute green linen with a thin belt and my talent dress would be a red knit I had hanging in my closet. Nothing to write home about but it would do. Mom and I did go shopping to find another evening gown, and we found a dress at Dayton's department store for $32.00 in black jersey, Wardrobe done ... I was ready.

There were 8 of us vying for the title. I was awarded both talent and swimsuit winner and then they called my name as the new Miss South Saint Paul! Thus, began my journey. Immediately after I was crowned one of my judges, Kathy Langenfeld, came up on stage and asked me, *"If you don't win State in June will you compete again?"* That was a confusing question for a 19 yr. old who knew nothing about the system. She explained that you could compete as many times as you wanted in the locals in trying to win the state title. *"Oh no,"* I responded, *"just this once I will try. I have other things to do."* The mayor of South St. Paul along with a few others were not happy with my winning. I was from Minneapolis and they felt a girl from So. St. Paul should represent them and it was in the editorial page for weeks stating people's disappointment. But the rules stated it was an open pageant. All I could do was to try to win them over with my focal point being I was in St. Paul attending college. I didn't tell anyone at school I had competed and won a local pageant. That wasn't necessary and was a completely separate part of my life outside of classes.

It's now December and auditions for the January interim opera, Aaron Copland's *The Tender Land*, would be taking place before Christmas break. Interim classes involved students from about four of the surrounding colleges, so many performing arts majors would be auditioning. After listening to a recording of it I decided I didn't like it and would not audition. It was a style of opera that I felt wasn't necessary to learn. WHAT? Little Diva! Who did I think I was? Dr. Forner, noticing I had not signed up for an audition slot, called me into his office and asked me when I was auditioning. I told him I didn't plan to because I didn't care for the opera. His firm and irritated response? *"GET YOUR BUTT OVER TO AUDITIONS TOMORROW OR I WILL KICK IT OVER THERE!"* Okayyyyyy! He scared me, SO, I DID! Glad I did too. I was given the lead role of Laurie and that would be my homework over break. Man, I needed to learn how to get over myself and really commit, even if I didn't like something. He knocked this little diva for a loop! I needed that. Getting a little too high on my horse! I was wrong and lesson learned!

Christmas break was now upon us and I had developed a bad cold with laryngitis. I was trying to learn my role by humming or singing softly and when rehearsals began, I still had very little voice. A visit to my doctor was warranted and it turned out that by trying to hum or sing softly while I had this cold, produced nodules on my vocal cords. I was under strict rules to not sing or speak the first two weeks of rehearsals and had to use a slate board to even express what I thought while acting it out! I was told that even thinking about the music or vocal line could subconsciously make me use my vocal cords without knowing! The cast was terrific and helped a great deal during this little set back and soon we were all having fun with the slate board.

As spring was rolling into sight, the Schubert Club Vocal Competition was here again, and this time, I won first place. It was a great feeling of accomplishment and hoped I'd made Adyline proud!

The year ended, and I was all signed up for next year's classes. It felt like I had some consistency in my life. All was good, I was having fun!

SCENE 2: MISS MINNESOTA

My sister Tody had competed for Miss Minneapolis years earlier winning the talent award and placing fourth runner-up. A few years after that my cousin Roxanne competed for Miss Brainerd placing fourth runner-up and swimsuit winner. It was then everyone started looking at me and saying you're next! I said *"Nope. No way. I'm too busy with school and singing."*

But as I stated earlier, and you now know, I did decide to compete and currently held the title of Miss South St. Paul! I was in St. Paul going to school and now spent many a weekend over in So. St. Paul visiting the sponsors of every store that donated to the pageant, shaking hands and thanking them in person, meeting them face to face, and letting them know I was grateful for their contributions. Very grateful because the clothing boutiques gave me a clothing item free, and that was a necessity for me. This was great training in learning how to put myself out there and not be afraid or shy in meeting people. I must admit I really enjoyed my appearances and most of them included my first runner-up to be with me! Some appearances such as Winter Carnival included all of us local winners, which was nice getting to know some of the girls before June when the State Pageant would take place. That winter I also met my first Miss America in person ... Tawny Godin. After seeing her crowned on National TV, she was a celebrity!

June was approaching fast. HERE WE GO! I say that because it must include my family and friends who were and remained so supportive and encouraging! In reality, I believe they were far more nervous than me ... because ... well ... I wasn't nervous. It would not be my career, just a competition to win scholarship money.

Austin, MN loved being the host city for the State Pageant and it showed as they rolled out the red carpet! Registration kicked the week off on Sunday, June 20th, 1976. Every day was filled with rehearsals, and/or appearances ranging from "meet n greets" at the Mall to public outdoor fashion shows. Everyone was excited for pageant festivities, and people from every corner of the city didn't disappoint. They came out for everything as did the press. My goodness it was exhilarating to feel the energy within the community! There was a total of 26 girls and the week was off to a fun start. We were housed with host families and my roommate was Brenda Laidley, Miss Thief River Falls. Such a sweetheart! Brenda was part of the trio that won Miss

Congeniality. A three-way tie with Brenda, Stephanie Nilsen – Miss Bloomington (who I am still friends with today), and Miss Northwest – Luann Ladeen.

Interviews took place on Wednesday inside the Ronald MacDonald Bus! It was pretty straight forward and nothing surprising until judge Larry Moeller asked me if the name Joan Growe meant anything to me. I said *"No."* It bothered me enough to start asking anyone I came into contact with that week and hopefully keeping up with the outside world, *"Who is Joan Growe?"* I felt better when the backstage help and chaperones, I was asking didn't know either. But not knowing bothered me enough to ponder and think about it too much so I continued to ask everyone I could if they knew. I needed to know. All of us were so absorbed in Pageant Week we were not paying attention to anything political or in the papers.

Wednesday night before we went to bed, Brenda and I discussed our interviews, and before long, found ourselves crying. Tears that soon turned into laughter while asking ourselves *"WHY ARE WE CRYING!?"* No real reason ... just a relief of emotions. I since learned over the years that most contestants cry mid-week. Probably because interviews are usually over and done! Tomorrow would be the first night of onstage preliminary competition and we would be formally introduced to the audience.

Thursday evening came quickly and I would be competing in Talent singing *"Adele's Laughing Song"* again. When my name was called as Talent winner a wave of relief, happiness and gratitude soared within me. First and foremost, I was pleased with myself. I also knew it would please mom, O.B., and Adyline. Tomorrow I would compete in swimsuit and evening gown. Competition seemed to fly by Friday and to be awarded swimsuit winner that night was once again the icing on the cake. They never announce an evening gown winner because those points are tallied into the private interview points. They are the points that are held over to the final night should you make the Top Ten. As the second night came to a close one of the backstage hostess women I had asked about Joan Growe, came and told me she found out Joan was running for Minnesota's Secretary of State. Now I had that little puzzle piece should I need it.

Saturday morning arrived, and we were rehearsing for the final night production when the director came to inform us that before we would break for lunch, we would be having a second round of casual interviews with the judges. Two minutes allowed with each judge and when the bell rang, we were to move on to the next judge. They were seated at small individual tables spaced throughout the high school gymnasium. This was my opportunity to inform the judge who asked me about Joan that I now had an answer for him! When I arrived at his desk, he asked how the week was going etc. and I replied the usual *"Very nicely, the girls are great, I'm thrilled to have won two preliminary competitions, but I have an answer for you!"* To which he looked a bit surprised. *"I know who Joan Growe is!"* Job accomplished! Puzzle piece in place!

A short eight months earlier I started down this path of pageantry wanting to win some scholarship money not looking to win the titles or crowns, yet this night, Saturday June twenty-sixth of 1976, I am now wearing the crown and title of Miss Minnesota. The Miss America Pageant would take place in three months.

After the crowning everyone attended the after party and were full of congratulatory wishes but by this time, I was in a bit of shock and remember people talking at me with excitement on their faces as I seemed to only see their mouths moving and not hearing what they had to say! It was such a fun evening of dancing and gaiety, and eventually mom and I were escorted to a motel where we stayed up until the wee hours of the morning with excitement. After a few hours of sleep, we were escorted to the celebratory and farewell breakfast. When it came time for me as the new Miss Minnesota to speak, I cried and blubbered through it and I was sure I left everyone thinking *"I haven't a clue as to what she just said!"* Mother's first comment to me afterward was *"You need to pull it together and stop crying"*. Okayyyyy, note taken!

That first week as Miss Minnesota I stayed in Austin, Minnesota with our Executive Directors Bill and Darlene Schottler having official photos taken, paperwork and contracts completed, meeting with sponsors, getting a schedule of my first appearances and anything else that had a deadline to meet in preparation for the Miss America Pageant only a short three months away! I felt strange and filled with thoughts of WHAT AM I IN FOR?! All the while telling myself ... it's only a year out of your life or adding on the six previous months as Miss South St. Paul, a year and a half out of my life. Just enjoy it. The folk involved seem very nice.

That first week with the Schottler's went fairly quick. I soon realized what wonderful, lovely people were entering my life. They owned a huge pig farm, and it was beautiful ... even if when the wind blew the wrong way it didn't smell so good. A week later I was back home in the Twin Cities and meeting the entire Pageant Board. They expressed thoughts as to what needed to be done in preparing me for the Miss America Pageant. First suggestion from the board was to have my teeth shaven off to all be one length. Oh my, I had never heard of this before and what did this entail?! It sounded awful and painful. I had a small chip on my front left tooth caused years earlier sipping from a pop bottle. It didn't bother me and having won two pageants with it, might as well leave it alone. I told them no, I wasn't comfortable with that idea. I did have it repaired many years and a few children later when bonding came into the picture. No need to shave all the teeth.

Second, they wanted me to get a new evening gown. The soft blue chiffon wouldn't cut it for competition. I thought it would make mom a bit angry or hurt her feelings as she had found that dress just for the Miss Minnesota Pageant and I was sure must have cost a pretty penny even on sale, but she wasn't upset knowing I had a wardrobe allowance as part of my winnings.

Third ... change my swimsuit to a color other than white. *Why?* I asked. Their response ... no one wins in a white bathing suit to which I countered ... but I have won the swimsuit award twice in that suit. THAT was puzzling to me. Mom and I did go back to The Curtis Hotel to look for another suit only because I was told we had to have two swimsuits. One as a back-up. To my surprise the same sales woman that sold us the white one was there and remembered us. She had the same swimsuit in yellow and was sweet enough to sell it to us for twelve dollars as well. Success! I had my two suits.

Fourth ... change your talent song. *"Why?"* I asked. Because no one wins singing *"Adele's Laughing Song." "But I have won the talent award twice singing this song."* Now, I was not pleased but out of courtesy told them I would search for a song that would be as entertaining, show personality, and range, while still in the operatic category. I knew right then and there I was only appeasing them for the moment while deep down inside I knew the probability of changing my song was very slim.

Adyline and I went over numerous other selections and shared them with my parents, but we all came to the same conclusion that "Adele" was still the right choice. I told Mr. and Mrs. Schottler and our producer Joel Nelson I would take "Adele" with me to nationals because I was most comfortable with this song and felt if I could win two pageants with this selection, I had a pretty good chance of winning with it again. That became my goal.

It proved to be a busy summer traveling the state taking part in wonderful, fun appearances such as parades, local pageants, speaking at events, and promoting different Minnesota companies and sponsors. Traveling with all my chaperones and sharing those experiences with them, they become some of your best friends in a short three months.

One particular weekend of appearances I was with Marcia Herdegen. The weekend began with an engagement in northern Minnesota, almost to the Canadian border. We were having so much fun, laughing as we told stories, eating chocolate peppermints and M&M's melting all over our hands only to realize, hours later we were very low on gas. We hadn't a clue where the closest gas station was and worrying that we would we run out of gas completely before finding one? We were in the middle of a reservation with not a soul in site! Our laughter turned to prayers and a few miles down the road came across a gas station ... it was closed! NOOOOO ... how could that be? Where does anyone get gas around here? Prayers up again and now worried we would be stranded, not able to make the appearance, but worse how would we get out of this mess? Who would find us in the middle of nowhere? It felt like an eternity but a few more miles down the road, there in full sight was a glorious gas station! Hallelujah! After filling up the tank and starting down the road, we glanced at one another and slowly took to giggling about how silly we had been and needed to pull ourselves together. We made it in the nick of time.

We pulled up to the outdoor fair grounds, and I was still adjusting my crown as I opened my car door and leaped out! Marcia went and parked the car. The next morning, we were up early to begin the drive to the southernmost part of Minnesota for a parade. Here we go again! It was a sunny, clear day, and it seemed we were the only people on the road. I was driving, and speeding fearful we wouldn't arrive in time and sure enough suddenly there were lights flashing behind us. I'm saying to Marcia *"You've got to be kidding me. Now I've done it. Sorry Marcia."*

The state trooper questioned where we were headed. We began to explain our situation trying to look as sweet as possible all the while sitting in my Miss Minnesota car that has my name and title on it in bold lettering for all to see! Luckily, he let me off with a warning along with stern advice to slow down and get there safely. We did get there safely ... I just didn't slow down. I don't suggest doing this. We made sure to allow more time than necessary from that point on. Marcia and I still laugh about that memory to this day. Our memory.

Television and radio interviews were a given, but I always felt uncomfortable being asked questions. It felt very different than the pageant interviews. Some questions so personal and private, it made me squirm, but I was learning this is the press and they want to know who I am, what are my beliefs, and I, in return, was learning I was quite naive in many aspects and it felt like being thrown to the wolves. Many times, I would be asked the question ... who do you admire the most? Or who has had the greatest influence on your life? Geesh ... I was 20 years old and never given this much thought. Instinctively my first thought was the name of some opera singer or even my voice teacher but quickly, very quickly my brain would turn to *I had better say my mother or she will be extremely upset with me*. Lord knows I don't want her giving me a silent treatment or lecture on who I should look up to and how dare I not mention her. *Yikes.* After my first TV interview I returned home to mother standing inside the screened front door and before letting me in, kept repeating ... *"um ... um ... um"* while batting her eyes in all directions, this was my first lesson in NOT saying UM or YA KNOW between thoughts which was actually a great learning tool from her ... note taken.

The summer days were passing quickly. Mom, O.B., and their friends becoming more and more confident that I was going to become Miss America. They had t-shirts and buttons made with my picture that said **"We are Number 1."** At first it seemed so supportive and positive, and I do realize it was because they were proud of me, but eventually it became all-consuming and boastful. I told them to please stop talking about it in front of me because if I did not win, they would be the ones disappointed ... not me. I was prepared and knew I could and would represent myself in the best possible light and in return represent my State to the best of my ability. They did abide by my wishes. Then one day as I sat in the living room reading, mom entered and we started chatting. She pointedly asked me if I felt I would win Miss America. Even to my mother I couldn't say what I really felt because it would sound egotistical and she wouldn't be happy with that or so I thought, or was it because perhaps it would jinx my chances. My response was, *"My goal is to win the talent competition for my group. But let's just say I don't think I am coming home."* In my heart I felt I was going to become Miss America. That it was destined for me. Because Grandma said I would be. I also wondered if perhaps all State Representatives felt the same.

Next on the list was wardrobe. Luckily, mom was a great bargain shopper and the two of us started pulling together a wardrobe for all the rehearsals and events scheduled for the week in Atlantic City. My favorite was the blue ultra-suede dress we chose for the interview. It made me feel sophisticated and polished.

For a new talent gown, we bought a white gown for fifty dollars from the Bernhagen girls. Both Sheila and Pam Bernhagen had been Miss Minnesota and at that time the only set of sisters to carry the title! We had difficulty finding a long dress for the Evening Gown competition ... on a budget, finally settling on a black strapless jersey at a neighborhood clothing store. Not very exciting but classic enough. The dress needed hemming and alterations but would be ready for pick-up in a week. It was a good feeling to know that wardrobe was complete, and I was prepared to leave in one short week.

We returned to the dress store for a final fitting of my gown and hoping we would be taking it home and packing it for pageant week. As I donned the dress, I stood in utter disbelief. It fit properly to the body but what happened to the hem?! It was a disaster! There were areas four inches above the floor and waved in lengths in all direction. I spoke up and said, *"How did this happen? It was hemmed to the shoes I brought into the fitting. This won't do. How am I to compete in a dress whose hemline is all over the place."*

Their response was they felt they could steam it enough to stretch the shortest lengths. I had never heard anything so ridiculous. How do you stretch fabric four inches?! We left without purchasing the dress, hopped on a bus for downtown Minneapolis and went straight to Jackson Graves department store. Within minutes they produced a red sequin gown, albeit four sizes too large, off the shoulder with one long sleeve, called for their seamstress and began their magic. Knowing we needed approval of the gown from Darlene Schottler, the E.D. of the Miss MN pageant, we called and told her we had found a gown but needed to act fast as the dress needed alterations and of course we all knew I was leaving in a week. She immediately drove up from Austin, Minnesota a couple hour drive and met us at the store. She wasn't keen on the red sequin as Miss America Pageant had been known for the chiffons, jersey, and soft colored gowns. But times were changing, and we were on the cusp. She approved it and wardrobe was complete.

When I returned a couple days later for a final fitting, it was perfect. Like a custom-made glove. Toshiko was a brilliant seamstress and made sure everything was perfection! Jackson Graves became a great supporter of me and gave me a beautiful Sable Stole to wear during the parade and earrings for good luck! Yes, over the three months my world was definitely opening up and changing. Meeting new people and making new friends.

SCENE 3: MISS AMERICA

The day finally arrived for Karen Schaub, my appointed chaperone, and me to leave for Miss America! At the end of each day, it was great having someone to share and discuss the day's events. Once in Atlantic City you were appointed a local chaperone who made sure you and your hotel suite mate were driven to and from rehearsals and events making sure you arrived on time! Miss Hawaii, Haunani Asing, was my hotel suite mate, and we would be the only two contestants staying at the Sheraton Deauville.

Upon arrival at the Philadelphia airport, Karen and I noticed the bag that held all of my shoes was nowhere to be found. We had left it at the Minnesota airport! I had only the shoes on my feet. I would need to wear these travel shoes for orientation and registration with my dress? Oh well, not a life and death situation so I'd better make the best of it until somehow my shoe bag would arrive. Haunani to the rescue! She wore the same size as me and lent me a pair for the evening and next day! Finally, my small bag of shoes found its way to me. In reality, there was probably only three other pair in the bag. That first night we were treated to the Miss America USO Show. It was a fantastic and exciting way to start the week! It's all we could talk about the rest of the evening. This was exciting because if you didn't win or make top ten, there was always the chance you could be chosen for the USO show. It was exhilarating and something else to hope for! Phyllis George was in attendance as she would be the co-host with Bert Parks for the telecast. She was so glamorous, gorgeous, and dressed to the nines! It felt like we were mingling with real celebrities. Well, Phyllis was an international celebrity, so we were somewhat mingling!

I remember sleeping well that night and the alarm clock ringing early. Karen and I rose from our slumber, and the first day of rehearsals would soon begin. It was then, I realized I had forgotten my blue eye shadow. Yes, heaven forbid ... I said blue. At the time I thought it was a divine color! But let's face it ... it was not a pretty blue. Regardless, Karen Schaub went running around all of Atlantic City that day trying to find me blue eye shadow. You'd think my chances of winning depended upon that shadow! She was successful, but to this day hasn't let me forget what a goose chase it was for her! Oh, how we let the littlest things determine what is vital and important!

Tuesday was another day of rehearsals and the Boardwalk Parade that evening. There were thousands of people along the Boardwalk! Cheering! I'd never seen or experienced anything like it before. I wore the gorgeous brown Sable Stole over my white jumpsuit and of course the earrings they gave me for good luck. Those earrings I wore all week and eventually all year!

Wednesday, I had interviews because that evening I would be competing in Evening Gown and the two coincided with each other and done on the same day. Walking into the large room the judges were seated at a very long table with one huge chair in front of them for me to sit in. At first sight it was a bit daunting. The questioning began. *"Hello Dorothy, I'd like to know more about why you are enlisting in the Navy?"* WHAAATTTTT? Not me ... went through my head. Smiling, I answered, *"I haven't any intentions of entering the Navy. Perhaps you have me confused with my brothers or you have someone else's notes in front of you."* There was a scurry of papers and heads looking down, back and forth at the forms as we all chuckled. Ice broken!

The interview continued. I was asked about school segregation/desegregation and bussing, the comeback of musicals and the question I will remember always, coming from Jeanne Maxwell ... *"If you were at a party or gathering with family and friends and there was a knock at the door ... you went to answer it and there stood God, would you need to change anything you were saying or doing?"* I have always believed in going with the first thought in your head and gut instinct and I answered, *"No, because God is a loving and forgiving God who accepts us for who we are."*

The interviews were seven minutes back then and as I left and walked out the door, my companion from Atlantic City was outside the door waiting for me and returned me to rehearsal for the rest of the day. She asked me how I felt it went and I said *"I felt the questions were stupid."* Later that night back in the hotel room I recapped the day for Karen but as I was falling asleep, I thought long and hard about the questions and realized that not one of them was stupid. They were questions to find out who I was at my soul, the truth behind what my resume said, and exactly what I was made of. I learned later, when I began judging, the importance of every question posed to a candidate. How quickly she can turn from one subject to another. From a serious topic to a silly one. From one of difficulty to absolute silliness without looking like a deer in head lights caused from fear of the question itself. It shows personality, strength, vulnerability, morals, and the conviction of your statements.

As the first night of preliminary competition began and my group lined up for Evening Gown competition, I was confident my red sequin gown was not out of line. I believe it was the year of transition for gowns. There was a spattering of jersey, chiffon and sequin gowns and of all colors! We'd made the right choice and Jackson Grave's knew what they were doing in advising me to be bold and wear it! The evening ended with Carmen McCullum, Miss Texas taking the Swimsuit award and Miss Virginia, Pamela Polk, Talent.

I don't recall much of what we did the next few days except rehearse for the show over and over and talent rehearsals encompassing most of the time. I think we had a luncheon, and dinner or two, but at this moment in time, I only remember the evenings of competition. Tonight, Thursday, I would be walking to center stage and singing "Adele's Laughing Song" just as I had done at both my local and state pageants. My name was announced, and I was ready to achieve my goal, but all I could do was perform to the best of my ability and leave it there on the stage. That night I was named the Talent winner and would have been thrilled to return to Minnesota with that win. I was happy and content. The swimsuit winner for Thursday night was Miss South Carolina, Lavinia Cox.

Knowing I had accomplished my goal of being a talent winner anything else I could be awarded would be icing on the cake. It's Friday and tonight was my swimsuit competition. I had brought both the yellow and white swimsuits, of course, and pretty sure my state people thought I would wear the yellow, but I did not. Instead, I decided to stay with the white. I was now more confident than ever after winning Talent for the third time, with the same song. I might possibly have a chance in my white swimsuit for a third time, as well. The drumroll filled the hall as the first announcement for the evening would be swimsuit and as I heard Bert Parks call my name all that went through my head was WOW. I DID IT. AND IN THE WHITE SWIMSUIT! AGAIN!

I listened to my gut instinct, and it paid off. I now was a double preliminary winner. At this point I felt I would, more than likely, be in the top ten as I should have accumulated enough points within the scoring system unless I had totally bombed the interview and evening gown portions. Texas and New York tied for talent making Texas a double prelim winner as well, but splitting talent points with New York. The press and public thought we were the two favored to win. Saturday was the longest day. We never left the Hall because today's rehearsal was different. Today we would block for the live telecast and what would be required of those chosen for the top ten. Since there can be a lot of sitting around while production and television are making adjustments in sound, lighting, and everything else they are doing, you could find me sitting on the floor blowing bubbles with my bubble gum. Yes ... not such a sophisticated image for one competing for a national title, but yet a glimpse into a twenty-year-old still relishing her younger days and not feeling like a woman, or lady, quite yet. I was still a girl in college!

Later in the afternoon, one of the contestants tapped me on the shoulder and said there was someone over in the wings motioning to speak with me. I turned around and there was the most elegant woman, with the posture and stature of a royal. Though we had never met, I knew it was BeBe Shopp, our only winner from Minnesota. I walked to the side wing and said hello. She introduced herself as BeBe Shopp, Miss Minnesota-Miss America 1948. The next words from her mouth were. *"Dorothy, I have been the only Miss America from Minnesota and it's been 29 years. It's time for someone else from Minnesota to wear this Crown and Title and I know it can be you. I have watched you all week, and it's yours if you want it. Good luck tonight and I will be cheering you on from the audience."* WOW! What an endorsement. I knew my family and friends believed I would win but now I had BeBe's vote of confidence.

Ten p.m. Eastern time was approaching and Haunani came to give me a leaf for good luck. The only place I could think of placing it was in the bosom of my dress hoping it would stay put for the next two hours! The show was about to begin! Everyone was in their places for the opening number. I was in the wings, stage right, waiting for my moment to walk on stage when all of a sudden, the make-up and hair women from our dressing room, came to me and asked if they could trim the back of my hair and put a bit more make-up on me. I nodded and said *of course*. So quickly one began brushing and trimming my hair, while the other was applying eye shadow, blush, and lipstick. This was live TV. How sweet of them I thought, when really, they knew to get rid of that BLUE EYE SHADOW!

Throughout the hall, Bert Parks voice was welcoming everyone to the *1976 Miss America Pageant* and soon we were on stage for our opening number and then introduced to the world state by state. Bert Parks then began the announcement of the top ten, going on to compete for the title of Miss America 1977. One by one each finalist was called to the front of the stage. I was the eighth one called forward into a category only ten girls experience each year. This was the moment I knew to start anew. Competition points accumulated earlier in the week to determine the top ten are now erased, with the exception of the private interview. In under two hours, a new Miss America would be crowned.

Evening gown was the first phase of competition, talent second, and the final phase to compete in was swim suit. Before I knew it, we were in line for a final recap of the top ten and then straight into a commercial break! We stood there on stage waiting to come back to the live telecast! Thank goodness commercial breaks were only sixty seconds! Bert Parks walks over to the judge's box to get the top five placements. It began with fourth place, Sonia Anderson, Miss New York; she grabbed my hand as she walked past me to her place center stage. Next, Miss California, Linda Mouron. Second runner-up went to Carmen McCullum which sent a huge roar coming from the audience! It was to have been between Carmen and me to win. That's what the papers had predicted. Now, it could possibly be a great surprise. Lavinia Cox, Miss South Carolina was called as first runner-up. The remaining six of us stood there together. Marie McLaughlin, Miss Pennsylvania and also a fabulous ventriloquist turned to me and said *"Congratulations."* In my head I knew at that moment I would wear the crown, title and become the second Miss Minnesota to win. But I also thought ... oops, I didn't pay close enough attention in rehearsal today so would need to guess on what to do after I walked the runway! Well, I'll figure it out! HA!

The next words spoken from Bert Parks were, *"The winner ... of a $15,000.00 scholarship ... Miss America 1977 ... Dorothy Benham, Miss Minnesota!"* I walked to center stage where Tawny Godin placed the crown on my head and the scepter in my hands. I began to walk. The walk on that famous runway. That glorious, very long runway I'd seen many a Miss America walk, and now it was me. I looked at my judges and think I said or nodded a thank you and George Cavalier the producer standing on his feet clapping. Peering out over the audience, logically I knew there was loud cheering, clapping, and horns blaring, yet it was as if I wasn't hearing any sound, and movement seemed in slow motion. It's an unusual, surreal feeling and moment. I proceeded down toward the end of the runway; my thoughts were perplexed. When do I wave? Should I wave? Of course, you wave! Have I acknowledged each side of the audience equally? I see mom and O.B. being escorted out of the Hall. Mother is of course excited and in her usual manner, dramatically blowing me kisses! I reach the end of the runway, and stopped by the camera man on the moving camera dolly. There I see my cousins Roxanne and Suzy standing on their chairs enthusiastically expressing their joy at the top of their lungs!

My brothers were back in Minnesota watching from home. Sean ran through the streets loudly declaring I had just been crowned. Remember this was about eleven p.m., Central time and he probably woke a few neighbors. My brother Kelley was signing up for college classes Monday morning and as he said his name to the woman checking him in she asked if he was related to Dorothy Benham the new Miss America? Kelley replied yes and then said it was like being in the EF Hutton commercial where everyone in the room stops talking and there is only silence. The silence seeming very loud!

Meanwhile, I had an aunt who happened to be hospitalized at the time and was watching the pageant from her hospital room. She became so excited when I was crowned, she began yelling *"My niece was just crowned Miss America!"* The nurses just pacified her with a *"Suuure, sure. Your niece is the new Miss America. Suuure."* They were convinced she was delusional from medication adjustments! She said that story numerous times laughing about how funny it was when the hospital staff learned she wasn't kidding or in a delusional, euphoric state of mind!

But there was another very important family member cheering me on from far away and crying tears of joy in front of his television set unable to acknowledge his true connection to me to the outside world.

The camera man allowed me to remain at the end of the runway and accept the applause, but he soon realized I was somewhat frozen and motioned for me to return to the stage. Turning around, I moved as quickly as my feet would allow, and made my way back while the camera men were yelling for everyone to stay put and not move. I now was making my way up the staircase to the "bench throne". I wasn't sure what I was to do, so I stood for a short time then decided I would take a seat. Once we were no longer on live TV, the contestants were free to come over and I just remember Haunani standing there, hands on her hips, and a huge smile. That smile meant the world to me, and I believe she was proud of me.

The whirlwind began. I was whisked off to a very small, and I mean *really small*, room backstage. It was about three feet by four feet consisting of one little chair and a phone on a narrow shelf like table. I was told to sit and wait for a phone interview. They closed the door, but as I was waiting, my sister Tody had been escorted back to greet me and give me a hug of congratulations. I know now why she came alone, because years later she told me mother was mad at her for 'something' and didn't speak to her the entire week they were in Atlantic City. God, how awful. It was to be a joyful, fun week. Eventually I understood and understand all too well about mother's behavior when it came to the silent treatment. The phone interview was short, to the point, and before I really even hung up the receiver, I was being taken to the awards breakfast in the Adrian Phillips Ball Room. Hundreds, perhaps a couple thousand people present. I am introduced along with my court and brought to a table on a dais to eat with my parents and the Miss America President, Carl Fiore. BeBe Shopp made her way over to congratulate me and tell me how proud she was of my becoming Miss America. Minnesota now had two! We ate a great breakfast, people spoke, I spoke, though I haven't a clue what I said, and then it was time to leave. It's approximately three a.m. and I'm in a hotel room with Mildred Brick, head of the hostess committee, mother and O.B. and a few other people and Mildred gently removing the crown from my head. It had been placed upon my head with toupee tape and she was meticulously peeling each strand of hair off the tape! With live TV, using toupee tape was the most efficient way to save time when every minute counts. I said goodnight to mom and O.B. and as I did so, I told them that I wasn't sure what to expect or what the next year would hold but said, *"If they, the Miss America Officials, try to make me into someone I am not, tell me what to say, how to walk, how to talk I will give the title to my first runner up."* Inside I knew I would never compromise who I was and would remain true to myself, even with mother's critical, perfectionistic comments always in my ear and permanently in the back of my head. I clung to something one of my state judges, Larry Moeller, wrote to me before I left for Atlantic City to compete. Dated July 30, 1976 **"A Miss America is just like any other person so be yourself. Don't try to be someone else." Thank you, Larry!**

The last person brought to the suite was my boyfriend, Russ. He and his sister Ruthie were there and, in the morning, he would continue on to Pennsylvania for training camp with the Pittsburgh Penguins. At that point we wouldn't know when we would or could see each other again, but we were both off on exciting new adventures in our lives. There wasn't much time to talk, so it was a rather awkward and quick goodbye. I wasn't consumed with any sadness about not seeing him or even my family for that matter. I hoped this was going to be an exciting year, knowing it was a rare opportunity. I was probably also somewhat in shock. It's 4 a.m. and I finally get to go to bed, only to be up by six.

Sunday began with an early morning photo shoot on the balcony of Boardwalk Hall, a press conference and a farewell breakfast. I said good bye to my family and friends and was whisked off to a meeting with the board. Albert Marks introduced himself as Chairman of the Board and Chief

Executive Officer and spoke first explaining what the year would entail and what he expected of me. His words were comforting to my heart. *"Dorothy, we will not tell you what to say or what to do during your year. All we ask is that you remember who you are and what you are now representing."* I was at peace. I knew the year would be great. Some of us now piled into a limousine headed for New York City.

I remember a few people traveling with me, Peg McMahon who would be my traveling companion the first month, and Evelyn Baldwin the other appointed traveling companion, Bill Caligari the National Field Director, Carl Fiore the President and all explaining what would take place over the next week starting Monday morning. Bill had me call George Cavalier the Miss America show producer, and say hello from the limo phone. George hadn't a clue as to who I was and every time I said *'this is Dorothy Benham'* he would respond with *"WHO?"* I repeated this at least three times each time met with the same answer of "who" before I said *"Your new Miss America."* Bill was laughing hysterically by now and hence he nicknamed me "WHO-WHO." I loved it! Bill also had George confess to me a couple of other things such as, he hated my red gown and said I wouldn't place in the top 40! This was my introduction to the wildly fun, loving, protective family of the Miss America world.

We arrived at the Barclay Hotel in New York City, which became my home hotel the many times we were there. I felt like a celebrity overnight and treated like one. After a lovely dinner down in the entry restaurant, Peg and I were excused to our rooms. There were flowers waiting, well-wishing cards and a tin of Danish Butter Cookies. Peggy pointed out the tin and told me we would need to finish all the cookies by week's end because it's what I would carry my crown in for the next year. That task was easily accomplished! The first phone call to our suite was from Larry Flynt, publisher/owner of *Hustler* magazine offering me one million dollars to pose nude. I turned it down because there are just some things money cannot buy. A telegram was also sent and stated the offer was good for one month. I had framed that telegram but over the years lost it in some move across the country. I do at least have a copy of it.

Monday was an early start with talk shows back-to-back then shopping for over-seas size luggage allowing me to pack for two months of continuous travel and a carry-on piece that became the most important. It would hold my Crown, hair supplies, and make-up. If our luggage would ever be lost in transit, at least I would have my crown! I was also advised to purchase a small bottle of detergent because I would need to wash my undergarments in the hotel room sink! My shower curtain rod became my clothes line! That'll keep ya grounded! Tuesday was a photo session and these photos would be the cover used in the next year's State Pageant program books throughout the country and at *The Miss America Pageant* the following year. The rest of the week was meeting with clothing designers to pick out gowns and purchasing some wardrobe to begin my travels. I desperately needed a coat that would work in all temperatures for the first few months. I was given a beautiful mohair coat that I wish I still had today! I don't know what happened to it either ... maybe mother sold it as she did so many of my things.

Towards the week's end, another photo session was scheduled, but not until I was taken to Vincent Roppatte (known as Mr. Vincent) for a hair appointment that morning. We entered a salon and as we were escorted towards the back of the room. That's where I saw Jackie Kennedy. She was on her way out ... Mr.Vincent had just done her hair. I was next! What world was I living in?! Vincent Roppatte was known as the "stylist to the stars," such as Audrey Hepburn, Liza Minnelli, Grace Kelly, Judy Garland, Liz Smith, and Diane Sawyer. He was once quoted in a news article saying; *"Women don't get older, they get blonder."* I LOVE THAT! He didn't ask me what I wanted done to my hair, he just started working. Highlighting, cutting, and styling. I met with Vincent on numerous photo shoots in NYC and a few other hair appointments during the year and must say he was incredible and spoiled me for life. To walk out of a salon and know and feel that everything about your hair was perfection was a rarity. I always felt like a hair commercial leaving his salon!

The second week into my reign we began logging the twenty thousand miles a month. Every day I was on an airplane or two or three, with press conferences at the airport immediately upon deplaning, an appearance that night, and off to another state the next morning. Peggy always carried a jar of peanut butter and a box of crackers in case our flights didn't coincide with meal times. She was a life saver. One particular evening in that first month, we got off the plane as usual and straight into a limo to be driven to our hotel for the night. The hotel was a good hour or so away and our hosts had made dinner reservations along the way. We stopped at a lovely restaurant for dinner Peggy was seated to my right and after we placed our orders, she slid two aspirin over to my plate. I looked at her and asked how she knew I had a headache. She replied that she could see it in my eyes. That was the moment I knew I was in exceptional hands.

Peggy told me that my job was to enjoy my journey that year and she would take care of everything else. She said to consider her *"The lady with the stick who will not let anyone hurt you for I will beat them with my stick should I need to!"* She didn't really carry a stick! There were two Miss America traveling companions who alternated months. It was lovingly referred to as the "Changing of the Guard." My other traveling companion was Evelyn Baldwin who was a very nice woman, pleasant to travel with, and it was funny when she would fall asleep on the airplanes and begin to snore! But who am I to talk? ... I would wake up with drool on my chin!

One of my first and most memorable appearances was at the South Carolina Heart Fund Ball. A huge event where I would be speaking and singing. One of the women in charge of my appearance asked if Evelyn and I would wait in the ladies' lounge until it was time to introduce me and of course we obliged. It was a beautiful lounge, and I told Evelyn that I may as well take advantage of the facility while there so walked into the lavatory area and immediately a woman washing her hands turned to me with incredible awe and could not contain her enthusiasm of seeing me in there. She raced over, took my hands in hers, and began jumping up and down repeating over and over, *"Oh Lord, oh my goodness, I can't believe I'm meeting Miss America!"* So, there we were hand in hand now both of us jumping up and down, in gowns, and me with my crown on, when she abruptly stopped and trying to catch her breath, says in a calmer demeanor, *"Please don't go while I'm in here. I don't wanna think you do that sort of thing."* THAT became the story for me to tell throughout the year! One I will always remember with joy, humor, and endearment!

The first trip to Chicago was great fun and I would get to meet Jane Domurot the make-up lady for *The Miss America Pageant*. We stopped into her darling shop and she gave me lessons on how to apply make-up, choose colors of eye shadow, blush, and lipsticks that would match and coordinate with my clothing. WOW! DEFINITELY NO MORE BLUE EYE SHADOW FOR ME!

I was seeing our country state by state with scheduled store openings, pageants, parades, conferences, concerts, talk shows, even my first appearance singing at The Crystal Cathedral. Too bad we didn't have frequent flyer miles back then! In the beginning it seemed I was living someone else's life having security around me at all appearances, people wanting my autograph, being escorted around in limousines. Sometimes I'd ask the limo driver to pull through a McDonalds so I could get some french fries! But within a few months I grew accustomed to the schedule and what was expected. The little girls I'd meet would stare in awe at me and the crown asking to touch it and if it was made of real diamonds. The look of innocence, wonder and curiosity in their eyes was so beautiful. It made me wonder if I may be meeting a future Miss America!

The Minnesota state pageant directors and board were responsible for putting together, in one month, an entire "Homecoming" weekend of celebration marking my first official return to my home state and Minnesota didn't disappoint! The weekend began in the city of Austin, where our state pageant is held, with a formal dinner and show of entertainment by the previous year's Miss America USO Troupe along with Governor Wendell Anderson and other city and state dignitaries. The next stop would be in the city of St. Paul visiting my college, Macalester. I sang and spoke and again the college dignitaries honored and showered me with praise and recognition. The choir sang, and it was marvelous! Supposedly a few student protesters from campus tried to wreak havoc (throwing eggs) and show their disappointment in my winning a "Beauty Pageant" and not wanting their college represented by me but security whisked them away quickly. So, here's the deal, I firmly believe everyone is entitled to their beliefs and opinions but to this day it saddens me that some people in society feel the need to express theirs by disrupting the celebration, accomplishments, or lives of others just because it wouldn't be a choice along their path in life. For me ... this was the right path, and I had just been awarded thousands of dollars in educational scholarship money to pay for school. I was proud and no one could take that away from me!

It was always wonderful to get back to Atlantic City during the year and see Al Marks, George Cavalier, Bill Caligari and everyone who ran the organization and offices. They made sure to check in and ask how I was doing, and did I have any concerns. The first time I was back, I went to the office and saw Doris who was the traveling coordinator and front receptionist. She always made it feel like home when I walked through the door. Today she said *"Before you leave Dottie, I would like to speak with you."* I went to her before we left and she said, *"Dottie, your parents have called and requested to be reimbursed for any and all college expenses they have paid for. Is this something you want your scholarship money to go towards? Should I send them a check?"* I probably looked like a deer in headlights and I was a bit stunned. But what was I to say? NO? That would send mom off on a rampage. I responded with a blank look on my face and replied, *"Sure, that will be fine."* I was momentarily stunned and in disbelief but decided it best to move on and move forward.

Peggy or Evelyn would always answer the phone in the hotel room when calls came through and one particular evening, when the phone rang, Peg answered, turned to me and said *"Dottie, Mr. Bob Hope would like to speak with you."* I gave a hearty chuckle and said, *"Very funny Peggy,"* but she was serious. Mr. Hope was inviting me to join him in a fund-raising concert signifying the mortgage for his Bob Hope House in Cincinnati, Ohio would now be burned! The home for troubled boys was established in 1963, and Hope promised the founder he would come annually to hold a fund-raising event for the home. It would take place tomorrow! *Nooooo!*

Oh, how I wanted to participate yet sad to inform him my calendar was booked solid. There was no way it would be possible for me to be in Ohio between flights and appearances. Well, he just wouldn't take no for an answer. He sent his private jet for Peg and me the next day following my morning appearance and said he would have me back that same evening so I could catch my morning flight. It was a go. I packed a gown, my crown, and a little make-up into a carry-on suit case knowing after my morning appearance Mr. Hope would have a limo waiting to take us to the private airport. We were whisked away arriving at the stadium for the concert that was already in progress. Peggy and I were immediately introduced to Mr. Hope and his wife, Dolores. They were charming!

Mr. Hope asked what I could sing, the problem being I was not allowed to use my performance tracks because of Union rules and there was a live orchestra. I said *"How about 'Summertime' from Porgy and Bess?"* He said *TERRIFIC* and sent word to the orchestra conductor as I was whisked off to a changing room to don a gown and freshen my make-up. All I could think was, *do they even have music for "Summertime" ... how does an entire orchestra do this with no music ... will they follow me ... how do they know my interpretation?* I changed and was ready to take on the night all while my brain is processing ... this is show biz, no rehearsal, just get out there and wing it! Wayne Newton was winging it ... performing for 45 minutes, picking up every instrument in the orchestra and playing it! WOW! Just WOW! Cincinnati Reds catcher and baseball star Johnny Bench was there walking Mrs. Hope's dog as he too was part of this star-studded event and he would sing as well! Little did I know he was a decent singer! Then I heard my name and introduction while being escorted to the stage.

A huge stage in the middle of the arena with people all around me. It was packed! I looked over my right shoulder to the conductor, nodded, and he started the intro to my song. I began, and it was magically incredible! It went off without a hitch and that was my introduction to the real world of performance! I joined Mr. Hope two more times during my year. Once to christen his new airplane and another to be on his Christmas television show. Absolutely thrilling!

Just before Christmas, December 20 to be exact, I sang during the half-time show for The Liberty Bowl game and for some reason mother was with me. Perhaps traveling with me so Peg and Evelyn could have more time with their families for the holiday. I remember flying in to Tennessee with a limousine waiting and ready to take me to the field for rehearsal. I was handed music to "On A Clear Day" and needed to have it memorized by the time we arrived at the Stadium. Yup ... good thing I was a quick study ... just saying! It was such fun but cold. Not too easy to sing when the air is cold and crisp and you try not to visibly shiver while your body definitely wants to shiver!

It was right after that, I believe, I began my two-week break and spent the first week and Christmas with my family in Minnesota. I was taken a bit by surprise, actually horrified when I entered the living room and was met with a life size poster of myself! There were a few of them and in truth, larger-than-life size. I'm not sure if mom and O.B. thought this was a compliment to me or if it fed their egos. I'm going with the second option! Mortifying! They also decided that while I was home, I should do appearances for them ... free ... one for the real estate firm O.B. was now with, one at the church, one for mom's friends ... it was endless. Not much of a restful family break and honestly, I felt used ... taken advantage of ... or was I becoming ego centered not wanting to do things for free any longer? Was I becoming a bad person for feeling this way?

I stuffed my frustration down inside and left for Pittsburgh the following week to visit Russ and see a few hockey games. Taking his sister Ruthie with me, which was fun and also because in the few short months as Miss America, I felt I needed or should have someone with me all the time when traveling. At least in Pittsburgh I had a more normal break, whatever normal began to feel like to me now or would be again. Away from the busy schedule of being Miss America and family wanting everything my title could give them, this may have been the first time I realized anonymity was a blessing. In Pittsburgh, Russ was the star ... the celebrity ... not me. I preferred that.

The new year began, and I was back on the road meeting Pamela Polk, Miss Virginia 1976. We were scheduled to meet the beautiful Elizabeth Taylor and her husband, number six, Senator John Warner of Virginia. Elizabeth was sweet but very quiet and reserved. I do remember Senator Warren doing most of the talking.

Growing up, I had heard of Mardi Gras and seen pictures but never experienced it. Now my chance was coming into focus! It was in full swing, and I was scheduled to participate in the parade. Phyllis Diller was appointed The Grand Marshal. It was lovely meeting her and such fun to be with her at the dinner the evening before and the next day at the parade! The parade was very long and rather terrifying with hundreds and thousands of people all a bit wild in their behavior, throwing beads, candy and unabashedly approaching the floats. Passing through my brain was **where is security!?** It rained off and on as the wind blew ferociously throwing my hair up into my crown so it probably looked like Phyllis Diller's wig! I'm sure of this as someone yelled, pointed to me, and remarked questioningly, *"That's Miss America?"* The curriculum for the year was filled with new adventures I otherwise may never have experienced, and I relished being part of them while broadening my horizons.

Come June and July I was scheduled to appear at numerous State Pageants and relished in the thought of remaining somewhere for more than 24 hours. Some for a glorious five days! Five days! August arrived, and I was looking forward to spending my last month with six of my class State Representatives. We were the Miss America USO Troupe! Victoria Harned - Miss Kentucky, Linda Mouron - Miss California, Denise Davis - Miss Alabama, Teresa Lucas - Miss West Virginia, Pamela Polk - Miss Virginia, and Joyce McCormack - Miss Arkansas. The girls had been in rehearsals for a week before I joined them, so I had a lot of catching up to do in learning the song and dance routines. I would practice while they took breaks but within a few days of being on my feet dancing hour after hour my ankles and arches had begun to swell and I needed ace bandage supports to keep going. I wore them for the remainder of our rehearsal days and the first week overseas. Those fabulous state sisters would rub my feet at night as I kept them elevated. God Love'em!

We traveled to Japan, Korea, Okinawa, The Philippines, and Guam entertaining our troops. We would get to dine with and visit our service men and women after the shows. As we departed each base in our helicopters, they would stand waving and cheering with praises of thanks saying good bye. It became difficult to leave as many of them would hand us notes with a family member's phone number asking if we would call them upon returning to the states just to tell them they were doing fine. Bringing a part of home to our servicemen and women filled my heart with joy and appreciation. Appreciation for the opportunity to represent my country and never take for granted the freedoms given to me as an American. Ever. **EVER!**

It had been hot and humid, our costumes drenched in perspiration by month's end. When going through customs to reenter the United States, the customs agent asked Peg if he could open the trunk that held our costumes. We all gasped and began giggling when Peg said *"At your own risk!"*

We landed back in the States and with rehearsals already under way for the Miss America Pageant we jumped in to learn our show segments. My remaining time as Miss America 1977 was becoming bittersweet. I was ready to move on and forward, but was I really ready to be back in the world of everyday life? A changed young woman, without anyone to travel with or really protect me. Interesting how one can get used to being protected. For me the next year calendar had already accumulated numerous appearances. Almost as busy as my year of reign. I would miss my traveling companions and stopping into the office to see George Cavalier, Doris Kelly, Al Marks and the others who kept the office running. They had become family for me. My protectors. My life. I realized it was harder to leave them than it was to leave my home state and family a year earlier.

As the outgoing Miss America I opened the Pageant show singing and was in a few of the production numbers, so even my final week was wonderful making me feel very special and appreciated until the news arrived and I was told I would not be dancing the USO number with my state sisters! My jaw hit the floor! **WHY?** Why? Why would you not allow me to participate in that production number? It meant the most to me. I was devastated. Their reasoning being, it was right before my final walk and there isn't enough time to change into my gown all because the year before Tawny Godin didn't make it in time for her complete final walk. She was late. Even Bert Parks changed the lyrics to her farewell song to *"... she almost faded completely out of sight."* I argued my case and told them it was not fair and to let me practice my change. There was 60 seconds to change from my USO outfit into my gown, hair brushed and crown put on. Off in the wings, stage left, I stripped as a wardrobe lady was there to help me into my gown, Jane Domurot touching up my make-up, and Mr. Vincent prepared to do my hair and pin my crown. It worked. I did it and with time to spare because when you allow the right people to help you, it gets done. They agreed to my request!

Saturday night it all went perfectly fine! The USO number completed ... it was time for me to take my final walk as Bert began singing ... I walked to center stage toward the runway for my farewell. Waving to the audience and only thinking ... *my shoe is about to come off and I may lose it along the runway! My option would be to pick it up and keep walking with it in hand!*

September 10, 1977 just before midnight, I crowned Susan Perkins from Ohio our new Miss America 1978, and her year took off as quickly as mine had one year earlier. I knew exactly what she was experiencing and what the next year of her life would entail. The telecast ended and during the typical flurry of excitement onstage with contestants congratulating Susan and stagehands wanting to clear the stage area quickly, Al Marks rushed over to me and asked if I would return as a featured performer next year! YES! YESSSS! ABSOLUTELY! I had that to look forward to! For me that offer validated the respect I wanted and craved from those within the National Pageant realm! I was a good Miss America for the program and respected enough as a performer to be invited back. The Hall emptied and was now very quiet. I was all alone in my dressing room back stage, needing to pack up my belongings and change into my attire to attend the formal banquet when I heard a small voice saying to me, *"I'm here, Dot. I will wait for you."* It was Evelyn. Yes, my year ended as abruptly as it began. I knew Peg had to be with the new Miss America, but I never gave a thought as to who would be with me after the telecast and no one had spoken to me about this moment. I guess I assumed someone would eventually come and get me. So Evelyn and I packed up my things and decided we would come back for them after the banquet celebration, or at least by then I could probably have a family member help me. As Evelyn and I made our way out of the empty Hall and toward the Ballroom, a young boy standing at the top of the bleacher section yelled *"Hey mom, there goes the old one!"* Evelyn and I laughed at the truth of his statement. I was the old one and my year of reign was over! The next morning, I would speak at the breakfast and then hop a plane returning home to Minneapolis. I felt the exhaustion creeping into my body though my brain was still spinning on fast speed. I made it back to my parents' home before they did because they would be traveling in their motorhome taking them a few days to arrive.

Here I was back in Minneapolis and beginning the search for my own apartment. By now I knew there would not be any living at home with mom and O.B. For a few weeks I had time to relax and unwind before my schedule, that was booked solid with appearances emceeing pageants, and singing concerts began, along with fielding calls from companies asking for me to be their representative spokesmodel. Only a few days home and a call from Farmers and Mechanics Savings Bank came in inviting me to interview for a position as their spokesperson. We met, interviewed, and contracts were signed. This turned out to be a five-year relationship with wonderful people. Life was blessed and good!

Crowned as Miss South St. Paul

Miss Minnesota 1976

Miss America Registration

Haunani Asing, Miss Hawaii 1976

Miss America Rehearsal

Miss America Boardwalk Parade

Preliminary Talent Winner

Preliminary Swimsuit Winner

Mom, Me, and OB

Standing on the Balcony of Convention Hall
Overlooking the Boardwalk

Official Miss America Portrait Photo

```
ATA258(2321)(2-044528E255)PD 09/11/76 2320
ICS IPMMTZZ CSP
6142534957 TDMT COLUMBUS OH 22 09-11 1120P EST
PMS MISS DOROTHY BENHAM MISS AMERICA, DLR
CONVENTION CENTER
ATLANTIC CITY NJ
WILL PAY YOU ONE MILLION DOLLARS TO POSE NUDE FOR HUSTLER MAGAZINE.
CONTACT UNDERSIGNED REGARDING DETAILS. OFFER GOOD FOR 30 DAYS.
    LARRY FLYNT PUBLISHER
NNNN
```

Telegram from Larry Flint, Hustler Magazine

Three Miss Americas from Minnesota
BeBe Shopp 1948, Gretchen Carlson 1989,
Dorothy Benham 1977

Publicity Photo with Bert Parks

Bob Hope

Pamela Poke Miss Virginia 1976, Senator John
Warner, Elizabeth Taylor, Me

Mardi Gras Parade Celebration with Phyllis Diller

Crystal Cathedral's Dr. Robert Schuller

THE MISS AMERICA USO TROUPE

From the 1976 Miss America Pageant... from a year of representing their States and the nation... from an August tour of the Far East... they return to Convention Hall stage for the 1977 Miss America Pageant.

This has been a busy year and summer for the young women who comprise the Miss America USO Troupe. They began rehearsals mid-July on the fast-paced musical show produced by George Cavalier and choreographed by Marcia Hyland. They departed August 2nd with their traveling companion, Mrs. Peggy McMahon, for their Far East tour under the joint sponsorship of the Miss America Pageant, the USO and the Department of Defense.

They come full circle in their Pageant year as they are welcomed back to Atlantic City and the Miss America Pageant to perform selected numbers from their show... "I Got The Music In Me"!

LINDA MOURON
Miss California 1976

VICTORIA HARNED
Miss Kentucky 1976

DENISE DAVIS
Miss Alabama 1976

TERESA LUCAS
Miss West Virginia 1976

PAMALA POLK
Miss Virginia 1976

JOYCE Mc CORMACK
Miss Alabama 1976

DOROTHY BENHAM
Miss America 1977

The 1976 Miss America USO Troupe

Dorothy peers at North Korean positions
through a battery commander's scope at the DMZ

CBS Publicity Photo

Publicity Photo

Miss America Program Book Cover 1977

Kellogg's Advertisement Photo

Campbell's Soup Advertisement

Gillette Advertisement Photo

Crowning Susan Perkins Miss America 1978

ACT THREE

MARRIAGES / CHILDREN / PERFORMANCES

Entering what I will call the third act in my life revolves around the years I was married and divorced ... *three times*. It was a daunting task trying to balance a family life with some career choices for about 30 years. I will concentrate more on certain episodes dealing with the relationship between mother and me, my children, and career choices within this time period than all the details of the marriages and why they failed. That would be an entire book on its own!

My year of reign was over and I was back in Minneapolis. Russ would be leaving for training camp in a few days, so he took me out to dinner and proposed. This made me happy because he was my first and only intimate relationship and to whom I'd lost my virginity. So of course, I believed that was a substantial reason for marriage. I said yes and immediately felt a rush of fear wash through my body and mind. As we sat through an absolutely beautiful dinner all I could think was that mother would not be happy. O.B. would let it pass and have to calm her. I wore the ring until he pulled the car into the driveway.

I couldn't do it. I couldn't face my parents and explain I was engaged. I wasn't strong enough to have an argument. I gave the ring back to Russ and told him I just couldn't go through with it. I guess we broke up. I hurt him.

We had made it through an exciting year for both of us, albeit a trying year, and now I hadn't any courage. I was angry with myself. Why did my mother have so much control over me? I soon found my own apartment and moved out of my parents' home. It was a feeling of freedom.

Russ and I stayed in touch over the next couple of months, and we decided to try again. I flew out to Pittsburgh just before Christmas and it was great to meet some of the other hockey wives and girlfriends and attend the home hockey games. The team traveled one day during my visit but it gave me time to get acquainted further with some of the spouses and girlfriends. I did notice a small box that resembled a ring box on Russ' dresser wrapped in Christmas paper. I was hoping it was another engagement ring but scared at the same time.

When the team arrived back to Pittsburgh, Russ drew up the courage to hand me the little box. And sure enough, it was a ring. I said yes once again knowing this time I meant it. The next step was to call mom and O.B. and tell them we were engaged. As predicted mom blew up. The harsh, cruel words she now was spewing reduced me to tears. This was the first awareness of the dislike I had toward my mother.

I was always trying to please her, make her happy, overriding my own happiness and desires. This time I held my ground and stood up to her. I would not back down. Thus began my first experience of her silent treatments. She didn't speak to me for about three months and I became her new so-called punching bag. Tody was off the hook.

I began to plan the wedding without her, taking Russ' mom with me to look at venues and menus, cakes, even ordering the "new age" invitations without parent's names on them. It took a good month until mom eventually came around and asked to be part of the wedding festivities. One of her first suggestions was that I ask Kilyn Benham to be my flower girl. She was after all my half-brother Gary and his wife Judy's daughter, my niece. She was also the right age. I thought this to be a wonderful suggestion but it would mean them coming from Colorado. I was surprised and very happy when they said yes. When my wedding invitations arrived, I showed them to her and to her astonishment she realized the parents' names were not on them. *"Oh, you didn't put the parents' names on them?"* she said. *"No, I didn't."* I replied.

By September we were settling into married life. The hockey season was in full swing. I was making appearances throughout the country and the bank was flying me back to Minneapolis once a month to make commercials.

Finding a voice teacher in the area would be a task so I called Peggy Mulvihill to help me in this quest. Peggy worked in the office for the Pittsburgh Penguins and was like a second mother for many of the players. She and her husband, Attorney Meade Mulvihill, seemed to know everyone in the city or possibly the state!

In less than a week, she had a list of names regarded as the finest voice teachers in Pittsburgh. I decided to begin with the first name on the list. I proceeded to take lessons with her only to quit about three months later. Trying to understand what this teacher wanted from me left me confused and with pounding headaches. It was all wrong. Another forced method of singing ... I was done with that. Back to the list and on to the second name.

Bea Krebs! Head of the opera department at Carnegie Mellon University. We hit it off and her style of teaching was similar to Adyline's yet she pushed me further in vocal production. I enrolled at the school thinking I would finish my degree in vocal performance with her but, I had booked myself too heavily in travel and appearances. In the end, I was compelled to drop out and continued to take lessons from her privately.

Bea was so much fun! One Saturday as I arrived for my lesson she was laughing and telling me how the crown of her tooth came off and she took some Elmer's glue and stuck it back in her mouth. We had the lesson and then she departed to the dentist's office!

The second year of marriage found me pregnant having just switched from the birth control pill to using a diaphragm, my doctor was going forward with a pregnancy exam and then blood work saying he felt I was probably pregnant and declared *"The diaphragm works if you actually use it."* Excuse me!? I replied *"I WAS using it!"* Obviously not the best choice of birth control for me!

Since my year as Miss America, I had been a featured performer at the Pageant and scheduled to co-host along with Ron Ely fall of 1980. I phoned Al Marks and informed him of my pregnancy. His delightful response ... *"It's good for people see that Miss America's go on to have normal lives and babies!"* I would be almost seven and a half months pregnant when the telecast would take place and if I'm not mistaken, I believe I was and still am the only Miss America to perform or co-host while pregnant, but that could be disputed!

Mother came out the first part of November to be with me as Russ was on the road. Monday, November 10th I was awakened with a slight pressure and cramping in my stomach. I remained in bed for about an hour and soon

I was timing contractions. I called my doctor who suggested I come over to the hospital and be examined.

I was far enough along to be admitted, but I went home instead and told him I'd be back when the contractions got stronger. Labor was mild so mom and I did go grocery shopping with my having a contraction per aisle! When we reached the checkout counter the sweet checkout clerk asked when I was due. *"Any time now. I'm in labor as we speak!"* I replied! She began bagging groceries so fast it was comical!

After putting groceries away at home, Russ walked in the door. It was perfect timing as the contractions now were causing me to lean against the kitchen counter and start deep breathing ... off to the hospital again to have a baby! I had been determined to give birth naturally taking all the classes on "Lamaze" breathing so I could go without the help of any pain blocking methods.

This went on until about 7 a.m. the next morning, the 24th hour, when signs of distress were showing for me and baby. The doctors agreed to give me a spinal and get me into the labor room. Once in the delivery room the nurse told me to sit on the edge of the bed so they could give me the block in my spine! I replied ... through great pain and pressure and only seconds in between contractions ... *"I can't!"* That nurse firmly grabbed me, sat me upright and said, *"Look at me and breath, you cannot move while the needle is inserted, so start now. Start breathing!"* Her voice meant business, and she was scary! As soon as that spinal took hold, my first thought was *"WOW! THIS IS HOW TO GIVE BIRTH! NO PAIN ... NO PRESSURE ... NO MORE NATURAL BIRTHS FOR ME!"*

Tuesday morning, November 11th Adam was finally born, but there was no sound to be heard. No cry, and the nurses immediately took him aside and began rubbing his entire body. I kept asking *"What's wrong with my baby? What's wrong with my baby?"* Russ was shielding my eyes from being able to see. Adam's little body was blue, and they were trying to get his color and breathing under control. Finally, a hearty cry came from him and he was going to be just fine. The umbilical cord had been wrapped twice around his neck. Thank God he was going to be fine. He was an easy baby and an extremely easy child. I thought how great is this? I could have ten children if they were all like this! (Insert big forehead slap here!)

Russ was traded to the Connecticut Hartford Whalers in 1982, appointed Captain of the team, and me pregnant again. Though I was scheduled to perform at the Pageant in September, this time it would be too close to my due date in October. In September I did decide to audition for the Simsbury Light Opera Company because rehearsals and performances wouldn't take place until after the new year. Even after auditioning at eight months pregnant, I was given the role of Yum-Yum in *The Mikado*.

February 1983 rehearsals were underway and at four months old, our little Russell began cutting his first two lower teeth with the typical symptoms of slight fever, runny nose, and irritability. It was a Friday night, and we had a babysitter arriving because we were attending a hockey fundraiser. I informed our sitter that Russell was not feeling too well because of the teeth, and off we went.

We returned home to a very fussy baby. It was a rough night and by morning I was on the phone with the doctor's office, not sure who was on call for the weekend. They said even though four months was young to have the flu, I should bring him in to be checked. I bundled Russell up and by now he sounded like a wild animal howling in severe pain the entire ride to the office, which was further away than our doctor's. An unbelievable fear was in my gut. The waiting area was packed with sick kids and I took a seat in the far corner only to have everyone look at me while holding a moaning baby against my chest. One woman mentioned to me *"He must really be ill."*

Finally, a nurse called my name and we went in to see the doctor. A pleasant young man who had me sit Russell up in my lap facing him. He checked the ears, nose, eyes, throat, heart beat and he then proceeded to tell me he couldn't see anything visibly wrong with my son causing the fever or moaning, and I should take him to Hartford hospital for testing of Meningitis immediately. I'd never heard of this meningitis. What was it? As the doctor was explaining, Russell's left foot began to move side to side. Within seconds, his left hand began the same motion. The doctor looked at me and said, *"Give me the baby. Give me your baby."* Russell was seizing. The doctor began stripping all Russell's clothing off and screamed, *"I NEED AN AMBULANCE NOW! CALL ME AN AMBULANCE. ASAP!"*

He then told me to call my husband and have him meet us at the Hartford Hospital. I called the arena, where Russ was in practice, and told him what was happening, while I rode along in the ambulance with the doctor and paramedics.

It was a cold February day in Connecticut and Russell was now unconscious stripped down to his diaper as we headed to the ambulance.

His little body filled with something causing him to have a high temperature and slip into a coma. The doctor left his office with a full waiting room of patients to be with us. The reality of how serious our situation was was hitting me. I was calm, and trying to absorb everything I was hearing and concentrate on the numerous questions I was being asked about my pregnancy, my health, dietary habits, the baby's health, his birth ... as all this information was being radioed ahead to the hospital so they would be ready for his arrival.

My neighbor was at the house watching Adam and ended up keeping him all day and through the night, if I remember correctly. That's all a blur to me now. Ambulance sirens were on and I know we were traveling as fast as allowed down the freeway but it sure felt like a longer drive than I had expected.

There was a group of nurses, doctors, and medical professionals waiting for our arrival as the doors opened and they whisked my baby Russell away for testing. Russ was there and we were guided into a very tiny room with three chairs and no windows. We sat in the chairs side by side silently. Of course, it felt like hours before the doctor came back to tell us what was going on and life seemed to be playing out in slow motion. The young doctor who left all those other parents and their sick children in his office waiting room eventually entered into the tiny room.

As he sat down in the only other chair directly across from us, he looked straight at us, then down at his feet, taking in a deep breath and then lifting his head to look us in the eye and said, *"This may be fatal. He's very sick. We think it may be spinal meningitis and he may not make it through the night."* The doctor proceeded to explain they did not know what strain of meningitis, so the doctors were going to take a chance and start him on an antibiotic to be safe.

Russ was placed in an isolated room with every precaution taken to not spread it or make his condition worse. We were finally taken upstairs to see him, and our hearts sank. Our baby was lying there helpless and in pain. There was nothing more we could do. He was in the best hands. He was also in God's Hand. That's where I put my pain, heart, and faith. I had to.

We went home around eleven that evening and made a few more phone calls to family and a couple of other people we felt should know and who would be able to help. Within twenty-four hours, there was a national prayer group in place for Russell. The next day they confirmed that Russell had Pneumococcal Meningitis. A rare form and must have caught a pneumonia germ from someone. The only person we knew who had just had pneumonia was our babysitter. We didn't blame her but she probably came back to babysit too early or didn't start her medication in time, or hadn't been on it long enough, I don't know. All I knew was my baby was fighting for his life and still in a coma. It was Sunday. The hospital and doctors were remarkable.

Russell had a neurologist, infection specialist, ENT specialist and every general doctor as well. They also found strange mucus in his ears and had it cultured. Something they'd never seen before and never were able to explain. Our doctors were very honest with us and something I greatly appreciated. The infection specialist was frank and said that *"If" Russell awakens from his coma we must be prepared for him to be blind, deaf, dumb, paralyzed from the neck down and/or all of the above.* In other words, back in the day, he could be known as a vegetable.

First thing Monday morning our pediatrician, Dr. Margaret Vacek phoned. She had been brought up to date over the happenings and said she would stop in every day to check on Russell. The phone rang early Tuesday morning with Dr. Vacek exclaiming, *"He's awake! Russell woke up today!"* What a wave of relief went through my body. I told Russ to go to hockey practice and I would head to the hospital.

All the doctors were in Russell's room discussing the progress, and whatever else doctors talk about in a circle, off to one side. I was standing beside the crib when all of a sudden it began again. This time on his right side. First his foot then the hand, and the rolling of the eyes. No sooner had he emerged from a coma he was seizing again. I ran over to the doctors and said *"Excuse me, he's seizing."* They moved like lightening. Whisking Russell away again for CAT Scans. I was told to wait.

I left the room and went down the hall to the waiting room. Soon a hospital chaplain came in and asked if I needed to talk. I thanked her but told her, *"No, right now I don't believe so. My son's life is in God's hands, but thank you."*

I wanted to be alone. Alone to pray and meditate. Within the hour Russell was brought back. The doctor's baffled saying they found nothing and he was awake again. They left to continue their rounds for the day with the exception of the infection specialist. He stayed with me as I sat by the crib holding Russell's hand. He said he understood what I was going through as he and his wife almost lost a child. Next, he looked at me and said, *"There is only so much we as doctors can do. There is no reason for your son to be alive except for a higher power." "I know."* I responded. *"There have been many prayer chains going throughout the country for my son. It works."*

Russell remained in the hospital for two weeks and we all took turns being at the hospital sitting with him and finally the day came when they allowed us to hold him. The nurses would put a pillow in our lap and then place Russell onto the pillow to soften any pain he may still be experiencing in his body. My neighbor and friend, Trish Whelan was an incredible help visiting with Russell for an hour or two, and helping out with Adam.

Finally, Russell was released from the hospital, and we were under strict orders to keep him in a two-month quarantine at home. No visitors allowed, no taking him out, and under advisement to wash our hands before and after handling him. My mother-in-law, Neva, came to help with the children while Russ traveled for hockey and I sang with the opera company. Her being there was a blessing. She was great with the boys and a fabulous cook with hot meals prepared daily. I thank God we had the doctors and hospital that were put in our path. They were diligent in following up with both the boys' care and well-being as well as ours.

Russ was traded to the Los Angeles Kings, and shortly after moving to California, once again I found myself pregnant with number three. It's beginning to look like a pattern here. Traded and moving ... Dorothy preggers! Our third son, Ben, was born in the spring of 1985.

Within the next year, Russ decided to retire from hockey and the plan was for us to move back to Connecticut. I decided three kids were plenty. We settled into our new home in the suburban area of Hartford and I now had a role with the Connecticut Opera Company as Sonja in *The Merry Widow* sharing that role with another young lady from Minnesota, Karli Gilbertson.

Karli had a gorgeous voice and phenomenal technique! Karli introduced me to her voice teacher, Doris Yearick Cross who agreed to take me on as one of her students. Doris was pushing me further in my training and stopping me if pronunciation of a word was wrong, the phrasing wasn't right, sound wasn't correct etc. It took two years before I had a breakthrough in producing the sound and placement she required. That particular day, as I sang a German aria I kept waiting for her to stop and correct me as usual, but it never came. I finished the Aria, looked at the accompanist and then back to her. Her eyes were smiling but she was quiet as I stared at her for what seemed an eternity. Finally, a smile came over her face, and motioning with her hands in the air, palms up and said *"Now THAT was a goddess singing."* I did it. Now to hang on to this breakthrough!

I was scheduled to perform again at *The Miss America Pageant* that fall, September of 1986. It was also when we learned O.B. had cancer and was given six months to live. He tried everything from Chemo to radiation but died three months later on December 31st. The stress took its toll on all of us and I went down to 110 pounds ... Far too thin. This seemed to prompt mother to comment on my body, well basically my breasts. *"Gee, isn't it a shame you no longer have your full, round, beautiful breasts?"* Well gee mom, that is what happens after having children and months of being stressed. Long story short, once again she wore me down over time and I decided to have breast enhancement done. Perk those boobs up like they used to be. Not larger just perkier. Mother thought that was a great idea. So, summer of 1987, I flew to South Carolina and stayed with my friend Stephan Yearick and had breast augmentation. I flew home the day after, tightly wound and bandaged. Mother thought they were great! Once again, I didn't need to wear a bra giving a feeling of freedom and that year my gowns at Miss America fit great! The feeling of freedom soon evaporated though and I felt stuck with breasts I no longer wanted. It would take years before I had them removed. By the end of the year, I knew I was pregnant again. Yep. It happened. My due date was September 2nd, 1988. I decided not to learn the sex of the baby because it didn't matter. I just wanted a healthy child. It also would be my last child informing my doctor I would have a tubal ligation immediately afterward.

In the spring of 1988, I was back with the Simsbury Light Opera Company singing the role of Elsie Maynard, in *The Yeoman of the Guard*. Luckily the costumes hid my tummy as I was five months pregnant! On August 31, my agent in New York phoned asking if I could drive into the city the next day and meet with a casting director, bring a resume, and a cassette of my singing just for future consideration of an event that was in development. It was my first meeting with Jay Binder. It was early evening and dark by the time we arrived in the city on September 1st. Russ stayed inside the car while I ran in to drop everything off to Jay. I sat for a moment conversing with him and he nicely asked when I was due. I said *"Tomorrow."* It really was quite comical, reminding me of the check-out gal in the grocery store when I was pregnant with Adam! Quickly jumping to his feet, he shook my hand and thanked me for coming all while being escorted to the door! Baby didn't arrive on the due date and would be the first of my children to be late in arrival. Exactly one week later, on the afternoon of September 9, 1988, we left for the hospital. Mom and the boys were giving me hugs and

Benny said, *"Mommy, bring home something different. I want something different. I want a green baby!"* Mother of course was praying for a girl. She was born that night and mother had her tenth grandchild and first granddaughter. I told her we were going to name her Mary Kathleen to which she responded, *"I know you are naming her after me since my first name is actually Mary but, I have never gone by that name because I don't like the name Mary. It reminds me of my Aunt Mary who I never liked."* So, I asked, *"Then what would you like to name your first granddaughter?"* *"Mia"* she said. *"Then Mia Kathleen it is."* That pleased her very much. I was scheduled for a tubal ligation the next morning. Four kids were plenty.

Two months after giving birth I called my agent in New York and said I was ready to begin going out on auditions. I called Doris Cross as well and said it was time for me to start singing again. Only a couple of hours later my agent called back and said *"Jay Binder is still looking for a singer. Can you be in New York tomorrow to meet Jay, then to the theater (I can't remember which one) sing 'Somewhere' from West Side Story in the key of E Major and just in case bring dance shoes."* Sure! Okay! Dance shoes? That was weird. But I figured at this point whatever concert this was and however many shows there may be, it might call for a bit of movement in an opening number, closing number ... who knew? Not me. I said yes, called the closest music store that would close in forty minutes and asked if they had the music. They did. Begging them, *"Please don't close until I get there. It may take me thirty minutes depending on traffic but I will be there!"* I spent the rest of the evening memorizing the song trying to get the starting note to sound decent as it was really written for a Mezzo and I am a coloratura with thankfully a wide vocal range.

Since mom was still with us, I decided to take her into the city with me giving her a day out for something other than watching the kids. We hopped on the morning train and first went to see Jay Binder. He remembered me and said *"Gee you look different than the last time we met!"* I sang and he sent me off to the theater. I stepped onto the stage and one man was sitting in the middle of the theater. I introduced myself and he then instructed the pianist to begin. This man, I learned later, was Paul Gemignani. I sang the song and then Mr. Gemignani instructed the pianist to take it up a key ... up another key ... up another ... and so on. He was checking my range and continuity of quality, I suspected. He told me to go to the other building with my dance shoes where I would be put through a dance audition. Alright! Dance shoes in hand, mom and I grabbed a quick lunch, a taxi and headed over. The entire floor of this building seemed filled with what looked like a hundred people most of them in dance apparel. After a 45-minute dance audition, a slightly built, distinguished older gentleman came in. He did not introduce himself but I immediately thought, is this Jerome Robbins? I don't even know why I thought that except for his connection to *West Side Story* and the song "Somewhere." He asked for me to sing and then thanked me when I finished. Mom and I left the building and headed for the train station when I heard someone running from behind, tap me on the shoulder (yes, I thought I was about to be mugged) when he said, "*Excuse me. Sorry to stop you, but Mr. Robbins would like to hear you sing again. Would you be willing to come back?*"

I was right! It was Jerome Robbins. The three of us turned around and headed back. Mr. Robbins thanked me for coming back and explained that he would like for me to sing the song again but this time he would not look at me. He wanted to hear only the voice. This was actually great because then I felt like I was alone singing and not having to perform for one person. When I finished, he thanked me again. This time I made sure it was alright for me to leave the building! Mom and I got on the train to go back to Connecticut. It had definitely been an interesting day. As we walked into the house and as if on cue the phone began ringing. It was my agent. "*Are you sitting down?*" she said. "*No, I just walked in, still have my coat on.*" "*Well, take it off and sit down. You got it! Do you want it?*" "*Ok, what exactly did I get?*" She went on to explain it was to be the biggest Broadway Show of the year. I told her I wasn't sure and needed to call my voice teacher. My next phone call ...

"*Hi Doris, it's Dorothy.*" After explaining what transpired that day, Doris became very quiet before she began to speak. I was preparing myself for Doris to tell me not to take it if I was serious about opera when she finally said ... "*I have a confession to make. I did 800 performances of a Broadway show. You must take this opportunity as it's your foot in the door.*" Wow! I called my agent back and said yes. To which she replied, "*Fabulous. They wanted you to report tomorrow for rehearsal but I told them you had a family and needed another day.*" I sat stunned and shocked. What had I just done? How was this even going to be possible? This was a turning point in my life again. I now could claim to be a Broadway performer. An original cast member of *Jerome Robbins' Broadway!* I was now a full-time working mom of four. It seemed we had all settled into this new norm, but the heartbreak for me was having my three-year-old son, Ben, chase after my car, every day crying and yelling "*Don't go mommy. Don't go. Please don't go.*" What was I doing? Sure, I was home with them on the days we didn't have matinee performances but I was leaving my children six days a week. I wasn't there to read to them or tuck them in bed. Oh, the guilt. Such guilt.

Strain on the marriage was also taking hold. As much as I loved being part of this company, my family needed to come first and my health was suffering with chronic fatigue syndrome. I gave notice to the show and planned on leaving once a new soprano was found. I booked a few pageant emcee jobs for the summer and a couple of other singing gigs, which would be a much easier schedule to uphold. Our musical director Paul Gemignani was now auditioning sopranos for my role but soon he asked if there was any way I would stay until the show closed? He guaranteed the show would close by year's end. I agreed to stay and get through the last few months and to this day I will be eternally grateful I did. By summer's end, my marriage was over.

I bought a round trip ticket for mom to come out and help me get settled into a rental house and getting her back home to Minneapolis by Christmas. Trying to keep life seeming as 'normal' as possible for the kids. There is that word "normal" again. Divorce is something I don't wish upon anyone. Especially children. The boys cried. Adam took it extremely hard just yelling *"No,no,no ..."* over and over. Russell couldn't understand why daddy and mommy were not going to be together and one night as I tucked them into bed Russell said he hoped his mommy and daddy would get back together. Ben started calling me "Butt-head." Mia was too young to understand what was happening but my heart broke. Even mom began to feel the stress of not being in her own home. She began flipping out on me demanding answers to questions she posed, but answers I didn't have yet.

The show closed and I was now collecting unemployment and trying to get gigs. I did book a commercial that was to film in Florida so I was waiting for the details when mother went off on me again. She started screaming that she needed to know the details of the commercial shoot so she could plan to get back to Minnesota. I kept trying to explain to her that I hadn't been given the final details yet so how was I to tell her? I kept reminding her she already had a flight ticket to go home scheduled and to not worry. But she was enraged. What was wrong with her? It didn't end well and she stopped speaking to me before she even got on that airplane a couple of weeks later. She didn't want to speak with me over the phone or have any communication with me. All because I could not provide her information I didn't have.

This was not unusual behavior from her as over the years she would find one reason or another to give me the silent treatment even when she and O.B. would come for visits. They just lasted for a couple of days and were over such petty little things like having a differing opinion than her. How dare we not think the same as her on every subject. She didn't like for us to think independently. This time was different and lasted a few months. Eventually she got over this long episode and began calling me again. I realized soon after the make-up call, she had been speaking with one of my high school friends and told him I was going through a divorce. He wanted my number. She had always liked him so of course she obliged. Unfortunately, this began what I eventually called the worst mistake of my life: ***Marriage number two ...***

It began with the sympathetic yet friendly phone call. Expressing how sorry he, Mike McGowan, was that I was going through a divorce and asking if it would be alright if he called once in a while to stay in touch. We had been friends in school so why not? I'd remained friends with many people from high school. The phone calls were every night and then weekly flowers began to arrive. A trip to California, Florida, and one to Minnesota when his father almost died of an aneurysm. Within less than a year he asked me to marry him, and I said yes. Mother and Tody were thrilled! They thought I'd made the right decision so I must have. Right? As a matter of fact, the comment made to me was if I didn't marry him, they would send me to a shrink! Little did we know that I would end up with a shrink because of being married to him.

We packed up and moved to Minnesota. I informed the kids I was marrying this man, they had never met and did not know, and moving to Minnesota. How traumatizing! THAT was extremely selfish, yet as their mother I thought I knew best. How arrogant of me. Thinking I was in control, but clearly not making wise decisions. Red flags in the relationship began to present themselves before the wedding even took place, making me question my decision to marry, only to end up convincing myself that I was; being over reactive ... he didn't mean it ... things would change ... it wouldn't happen again ... If I worked harder I could keep everyone happy. Let's just say the "clue phone" was ringing and I didn't pick up because I knew what would be said and I didn't want to hear what it had to say. The truth ... my gut feeling ... leave now. We wed and I put my fears behind me. I'd convinced myself this was going to be wonderful for all of us.

Mother and I had a nice relationship and started spending a lot of time together. One day she started talking about my being back on Broadway asking if my agent would have a show I could audition for or does Manny Azenberg (producer of many Broadway shows) have a show? *"Really Mom?*

It doesn't work that way ... what makes you think I could be in a Broadway show at this time of my life while living here in Minnesota and the kids have just started adjusting to their new life? That part of my life is over. Besides, Mike wants a baby. That makes five kids." (Actually, six if you add in Mike's daughter from his first marriage) Her response was *"Oh I guess you're right."*

Two years down the road and once again mother is not speaking to me. This time due to a family confrontation involving other family members. Some innocently caught in the dust storm of the argument. I will leave it at that, along with my disagreeing with what was being presented to me and asked of me. God forbid I decide to go against their and mothers wishes/ideas! This made mother enraged and she began to yell at me, tell me how selfish I was and I started to yell back. She left in a huff. The other family members following. This time her silent treatment toward me would last six months. I would call and invite her to the kid's school events and offering to come pick her up, to which she always responded with *"No. if I can make it, I will get there another way."* The only child she really cared about seeing was Mia who was three by this time. I would call mom at least once a week telling her *"Mia would like to see you."* Her only response; *"Yes, bring her over."* Talk about odd ... every time I'd drop Mia off at mom's, the front door would open slowly with mother hiding behind the door so as not to see me or I her. Mia, in her little voice, would say, *"Where is grandma?"* I only knew to respond with, *"She's right inside, sweetie, behind the door. I will pick you up in a couple of hours."* Every. Single. Time.

During this six-months, I underwent a tubal reversal with a six-week recovery period and immediately found myself pregnant. Eleven and a half weeks into the pregnancy I was grateful to not be experiencing any nausea. So far, so good until we were involved in a car accident. We were on our way to dinner at the country club when a woman ran a red light hitting my passenger door. The impact was loud and forceful, jolting my body back and forth until we came to a stop. We were both dazed a bit and very lucky the firehouse was on the corner. Firefighters came running, an ambulance was called, police showed up and we all stepped out of our vehicles. No one was hurt, thank goodness. Or should I say no one seemed injured. I felt fine until the next morning when it seemed impossible to move any muscle in my body with it being racked with pain. Neck spasms began and continued for months but the saddest result was my miscarrying the baby a week later. There was after all an injured person.

NOW ... mother wanted to speak to me again! Well of course she did! Having heard through the grapevine I'd lost a baby. The phone rang one morning and it was her. *"Hi Dorothy, it's mother." "Yes."* I said. By this time, I really didn't want much to do with her and her childish ways but she proceeded to speak and ask about the miscarriage and that she would like to see me. Could I come over that afternoon. Sure ... I did so before the boys would be home from school and before I needed to pick Mia up from pre-school. This time the front door opened wide and there she stood with her arms opened wide as if I was to run into them and be grateful because now, she wanted to see me.

Well, I didn't run to her and I wasn't sure I could handle her personality swings any more. I said hello and suggested we go into the living room and talk about what's gone on for half a year. I told her I would love for her to be part of my life, our lives, but that over the years she had given the silent treatment too many times and I wasn't going to put up with it any longer. If she did this to me again, our relationship would be over. Her face in a frozen smile and her head nodding yes, I knew she wasn't comprehending what I was saying and that I meant it. To me it was obvious she wasn't listening. I had decided I didn't like her as a person and needed to try to love her because she was my mother. How could I not like my own mother as a person? This is the woman who raised me. Taught me to be kind, to not say awful things about another person ever. Say kind things about people. This was when I was struggling to know who she was and what has made her this way. O.B. was gone, perhaps she was lonely. Maybe she was alone too much. I don't know. So, we went back to doing things together and my trying to keep her entertained.

I conceived shortly after the miscarriage and due to my age of thirty-eight given an amniocentesis but decided against knowing the sex of the baby. We talked about names for the baby knowing that if it were a boy, more than likely he would be named after Mike's father. If it was a girl we vacillated on names. I told mother one of the girl names we were contemplating was Madeline ... Maddie for short. She then responded with *"How about Mary?"* My head wanted to spin around like a top when she said this but I gathered my senses and responded calmly with *"Mom, you didn't want Mia named Mary because you told me you hated the name Mary because you didn't like your Aunt Mary. Why would you now want to name a girl, if it's a girl, Mary?"* *"Oh, that's right"* she said. Aye-yi-yi !

This pregnancy continued smoothly with a very active baby inside of me. I would joke about having a spirited child and maybe we should prepare ourselves! The wee hours of April 20th arrived and baby decided to make an entrance! The epidural only took hold on half my stomach but it was doable so I chose against having another. Baby's little chin was stuck on my tailbone and the doctor knew either he needed to break baby's chin or my tailbone. He made the right choice in breaking my tailbone! The little head emerged already screaming! Yes, this may definitely be an active, determined child. In minutes we had a beautiful, (or exquisite, as my mother remarked) dark haired baby girl. She proved to be a very active baby, and child with one pediatrician commenting *"My, she's rather a whirling dervish, isn't she?"* To which I replied, "Oh, *this is calm for her!"* Let it be known she still is and I love it! She was the first blessing to come from this union.

Life was busy as a mom of five and keeping up with everyone's homework and schedules but the plan was to have one more baby quickly before I turned forty. A few months after Madeline was born, I found myself pregnant with number six, craving Burger King Whoppers, fries, onion rings and beer. Of course, I didn't drink the beer but found it so unusual as a craving as I don't even like beer! Since there was to be another amniocentesis, we decided to learn the baby's sex but not tell anyone. We knew it would be a boy.

June of 1995, our son Richard was born and we had Irish twins! He was the second and final blessing from this union. For the next few years, I carried them around, one on each hip and will say it was a daily work out. Who needed a gym membership! Thank goodness for the older kids who were a great help in caring for their two youngest siblings.

Summer months found us at the Lake cabins. Spring breaks on Sanibel Island, Florida at the family beach condo. Country Club neighborhood, Country Club membership, political fundraisers and parties, jewelry ...

Life **'appeared'** good.

Being a mother of six and a wife took all my energy and I no longer had an identity as Dorothy Benham, singer, musician, performer. It was a decision I'd made and accepted even knowing a part of me was not being fed. The part of me that began by the time I was two years old.

I'd decided I would never sing again until the day my phone rang a few times. Phone calls from Pastor Youngdahl, the choir director, and the music director at church all asking if I would come sing in the Senior Choir and be the soprano section leader. It was a paid position and would give me the opportunity for performance once again. I had to give this a lot of thought because I wasn't sure how that would fit into my life but eventually concluding maybe I should be doing more. Something for myself. Something that nurtured my musical abilities making me feel I still had something to offer through music. I told Mike about the phone calls and that I was going to take the position. His response was cool and he said *"Really."*

He obliged to this three-hour Sunday schedule for a time but eventually dwindling to me and the children attending by ourselves. I never felt one hundred percent supported in this decision and the next four years brought things I'd not experienced before. Feelings of insignificance. Worthlessness. Doubt. Sadness. Privately, tears came easily and so it began ... the beginning of the end. It was a Thursday and he asked if I was going to be home the following day, to which I replied yes. He said *"You are going to be served divorce papers."*

The week following was so strange. I felt outside of my body just trying to keep the wheels moving and trying to hide any and all emotions I was feeling from the kids. I was moving through the days like a robot trying to make things "appear normal" hoping the kids didn't suspect anything. Kids know everything. The divorce papers were served and I went over to Pastor Youngdahl, for guidance. Basically, there wasn't anything that could be done.

The next week took a dramatic toll on me. I was not eating or nourishing my body, only concentrating on the children and their needs. The following week I collapsed. I went to mom's condo to talk with her on that Tuesday night and I became inconsolable and unable to stop crying. Tired. I was so tired. Just so very tired. We went to the hospital emergency room and they gave me IV fluids for dehydration. I felt so much better! The crying stopped and even though I was exhausted, I felt clear-headed and only wanted to go home. They told me they would keep me overnight and I assumed in a regular hospital room. Obviously, my mother convinced them it wasn't safe for me to go home so they admitted me to the psych ward. WOW! They take everything from you. Jewelry, shoes, anything they think you could harm yourself with including the wrist brace I had on!

The sprained wrist happened one month earlier when I was putting laundry away one day, and tripped over the foot of a bed. My cleaning lady was at the house with me when that happened and agreed to keep an eye on the two youngest kids while I ran to get an x-ray. Mike was furious I had gone quickly for an x-ray and not called him so he could accompany me. For crying out loud ... it took an hour and then I was back and waiting for the other kids to get home from school. Anyway, the hospital room was cold and sterile. But I thought, now I can sleep. Wrong. There wasn't much sleep that night as they sent in a psychologist who gave me a test for domestic abuse. Upon completion she looked at me and said *"You have been in an abusive relationship."* She stayed for about another hour just talking to me. I appreciated that conversation but just wanted to sleep. She left and I tried drifting off but was soon interrupted by my doctor coming through the door. It was a relief to see Dr. Boardman. He had been my doctor since my college days and knew me well.

We picked up on a suggestion he had given me a month earlier when I saw him for my sprained wrist. At that time, his intuition and the change in my personality told him I was in some kind of abusive relationship. This time I agreed. We talked about different medications I should probably go on for a while until all of this played out and life could take a gentler path. A few hours passed but sleep was now difficult. Morning arrived and my Pastor, Pastor Youngdahl was next to walk in and give me his support. I cried quietly with him. He understood.

What a trip to be in a psych ward. Lot's going on in that department and I was happy to leave. The group session was an eye opener and definitely interesting when you realize most of the patients in there knew one another. Guess they were regulars. Luckily after two days they released me and Friday I flew off to New York with Mia. I was commentating a Halloween costume segment for NBC, and Mia was modeling. We returned Sunday and that evening after putting the two youngest to bed I told the older kids Mike had served me divorce papers. We were all crying by now and angry. After much conversation of what everyone endured over the last five years, Adam piped up and said, *"Well, if it teaches us anything, it's how not to treat people."* Amen to that!

I continued to sing in the choir, for funerals and weddings, and then became the front office receptionist for the church. It was a busy schedule to keep while being a mother of six but it kept a roof over our heads and food on the table. Luckily mom helped out during the week with Madeline and Richard. They were so young yet, just kindergarten and preschool. Mom didn't drive, which meant I picked her up before the kids went off to school, then got them out the door, and I left for work. On my lunch break I would pick Richard up from pre-school and take him home only to have mom in the doorway with her coat on saying she wanted to go home and Richard would need to go with her. Richard would cry softly to me and say *"I just want to stay home mummy."* It was a juggling act keeping everyone somewhat happy.

Number Three:

I met my third husband through a mutual friend about a month after my second divorce was finalized. Again, I rushed into a relationship thinking I'd found the right partner. He was mild-mannered, liked music, and was the son of a minister. I thought we had a lot of common interests. We made my first CD recording together (mother really liked that) but soon it became clear she was jealous of my spending extra time with him as we put together a second CD of Christmas songs and started putting together a Christmas concert at Orchestra Hall. By the time I recorded my second CD she was pulling away and not wanting to speak with me and showing no interest in the new recording. The silent treatment was beginning again. I had told her years earlier if she gave me the silent treatment again, I would not put up with it. It drained me. I no longer had the patience to deal with her. The decision was made and so began a decade plus of my eliminating her from my life.

During this time period, I was reintroduced to The Crystal Cathedral – *Hour of Power*. We sent them my first recording of sacred songs and they invited me out to sing. It was the beautiful beginning of two decades of my being a featured musical guest artist. I lived for the next time I would be invited to sing and there were many, ranging from the church services, to special concerts and tributes, to tree lighting ceremonies. I never wanted to leave because my heart and soul were filled with a happiness and grace I'd not experienced elsewhere. This was an opportunity of working alongside incredible musicians, making lifelong friends, and feeling pure joy from every person associated with the church and also the congregation. What a blessing.

Two years into the relationship we were married. I was still singing at funerals and weddings and that provided some income for me along with the sales of the CD's for a while. January of 2005 began with my having frozen shoulder, then a hysterectomy. Surely the remaining six months of the year had to be better. We decided to open a bridal/pageant/prom dress store called Dorothy Benham Bridal, but I found myself needing neck surgery just before we opened. Got through that alright then only to be misdiagnosed with rheumatoid arthritis and put on prednisone and eventually another medication to ease off of the prednisone. Before long I felt this diagnosis was incorrect and went off all medications. Sure enough, I was right. I was fifty years old and feeling it. Feeling I needed to take better care of myself and stay in tune with my body.

I ran the dress shop for three years and that took a huge toll on me and my family. I would open the store, work all day, run home to make dinner and then many a night be back to the dress shop for private appointments. Laundry was usually done at midnight. It was rough so we closed that down. The other part of life that was slowly closing down was the marriage. After six years of being together, we were only roommates, no intimacy, very little conversation. At the time, I presumed this is what happens. We get older and life continues on a day-to-day basis of just being. Rather boring and I believed this is how my last years would continue. Just surviving. Money felt tight and toward the ninth-year of marriage delinquent financial notices began to arrive for a few accounts. But they were big accounts. My name was on everything and I was furious. Not only at him but also myself for not staying on top of the finances the way I should have. I should not have put full trust in someone. When I began to ask questions, he lied right to my face. Ten months were spent sneaking around getting as much discovery work done as possible and it felt horrible. I hated having to look for things in private. When I felt I had enough to present to an attorney, I did so and filed for divorce.

Relationships are fragile and when combined with abuse, substance abuse, lies and deception, lack of respect and support, it leads to a complete break down and for me, divorce. I'm not proud of this track record and have been embarrassed by it until recently. I take ownership and responsibility for my part in them. Many lessons learned.

Divorce is an ugly animal and I do not wish it upon anyone.

First Rehearsal with Jerome Robbins

PLAYBILL

IMPERIAL THEATRE

Jerome Robbins' BROADWAY

Kilyn and Me

Madeline, Russell, Me with Richard on my lap, Ben, Mia, and Adam

FINALE

SCENE 1: SHE'S GONE

I began to feel alive again embracing each day with a new found joy, and learning to love myself.

Over time, I reconciled with mom and I no longer had the strain of raising kids. They were grown and out of the house. The first two years with mom were good, actually great with time to shop and dine, or take in a concert here and there in the evenings after my work and of course the weekends. Mom's health was okay, but followed very closely by her doctors. Especially her heart doctors.

She wasn't feeling well one evening and went to bed early. Her coloring was off and I told her I would call the doctor in the morning if she wasn't better. By five a.m. I heard her moaning and went in to check on her. She had a slight fever and was shaking with chills. I tucked her down comforter around her, got her some ginger ale and said I'd be back in about thirty minutes to check on her again. I fell asleep and woke about an hour and a half later and jumped out of bed, mad at myself for having fallen back asleep. I ran into her bedroom and she was incoherent and disoriented. Her coloring was a whitish gray. Immediately, I called 911 for an ambulance and then I called my brother, Kelley.

They took her to the hospital where she was diagnosed with the E. coli infection. Her body was never able to combat this infection and like clockwork it raised its ugly head every six weeks. She would usually need a PICC line and go into the hospital every day for two weeks for an infusion of antibiotics.

Every once in a while, oral antibiotics worked, but again it was a balancing act deciding which would work along with all of her other medications. Now, when her friends would call and ask how she was doing her response was always *"Oh, I have Ebola again. Oh, no? Wait, Dorothy says it's not Ebola it's E. coli."* That became our joke for the next two years.

Between my brother Kelley and his wife Judy, we were able to keep her in her home. Mom was gentler with me now and thanked me every day for helping her and being with her. Mother also seemed to have grown a sense of humor that I never saw in her before. At one point, she fell in lust with her infection specialist, Dr. Sanchez, and blatantly told him if she were 30 years younger, he wouldn't have a chance! WOW! Who was this woman? This was a wilder, over the top, outspoken, toss it to the wind, carefree attitude I'd never experienced with her. Well, unless you count her celebrity crushes on Clark Gable and Placido Domingo! We sure had some cute chuckles over her crush because she had to make sure her lipstick was on and her hair wiglet pinned in just right before she saw him.

Between her vanity and pride, she fought us every inch of the way when it came to using a cane, a walker, and then to a wheel chair, and definitely did not want to wear a life alert necklace. Even though I told her I would bedazzle it for her! Eventually she succumbed to all of the above. Water retention pills played a huge part in keeping her healthy and it was a delicate balance.

I would stop by before work in the mornings to get her vitals and call the doctor. But one morning her coloring was off and she didn't feel well. I put her to bed and reported this to the doctor. It was recommended that mom try to stomach any of her medications that she could during the day. She wasn't able to stomach them. And there were many pills a day to take. That alone was difficult. Kelley and Judy checked in on her and I went straight over after work. She seemed MUCH better and we were all relieved. The next morning, I did the usual and stopped by for our regular routine and she was perky!

I was seated at her dining table adjusting her daily medications when she piped up and said in a very coquettish way, *"I have a confession to make."* "Ok," I said. *"I told Bernice* (her best friend who had been a nurse) *what I did yesterday."* I'm looking at her with puzzlement because what can a ninety-year-old woman do without one of us finding out?

She can't go anywhere by herself. We are always around her. *"Well, yesterday I took an extra water retention tablet. The one in the cupboard. Not my usual."* Now I'm looking at her with disbelief, staring at her and I repeated *"The extra strength pill that is ONLY prescribed by the doctor if your weight goes five pounds or over in one day? WHY? Why on earth would you do that? Your medication is a fragile balancing act. Sometimes you only get half a one. Only your doctor can decide when that pill is needed. You could have killed yourself. You almost did! Now I need to call Sandy."* Sandy is the Physician Assistant Certified at the Preventive Cardiology Clinic in Minneapolis. It was Sandy who mother trusted. The woman who, in our opinion, through medication adjustments kept mother alive.

"Why, mom, why would you have taken that medication? I need to tell her what happened so she knows what to look for over the next few days!" I was flabbergasted! I'm sure you are wondering what her response was to my asking why? ... Standing behind her kitchen counter and coquettishly she replied with *"I don't know. I guess I just wanted my ankles to be thinner."* HA! Ha,ha,ha,ha,ha,HA! Her vanity came through again. She was worried about her swollen ankles and almost killed herself. She pleaded with me not to call Sandy but I had to. I needed to know how to adjust her medications. I left a message with Sandy's nurse, Angela. Now Angela and I became morning coffee clutch pals over the two years because I would report mom's statistics five days a week to her, then she would inquire with Sandy.

While we waited for Sandy's phone call, I took mom shopping at the mall. Pushing her in her wheelchair I started to giggle and she said, *"What are you giggling about?"*

"Mom, I'm trying to find a little humor in what you did and here is what I am going to do just for you. When you die and we have a viewing of your body, I'm only going to present your ankles. Only the bottom half of your casket will be open to display your lovely, thin ankles!" *"Oh, that's just terrible,"* she said and then laughed. We laughed, knowing full well she didn't even want a viewing. It had scared us both and the laughter made it bearable. Sandy reassured us all would be fine and tomorrow we would start again but we decided I could not keep that bottle of pills at mom's house. Those now stayed with me.

She had wonderful doctors who worked together and kept her alive until her body just wasn't able to handle any more. They guided me through every step and what to expect so that I could relay all of her treatment to my siblings.

We were all grateful for the care and friendship they gave to her. Her last month she was put on hospice, and Tody and Bob came to help for a month. Bob was in the throes of dementia and Tody had her hands full with him, too. Tody kept busy cooking and trying to keep mom fed until the last week when mom told me she just wasn't hungry and didn't want to eat.

"Tody. You can stop cooking. Mom doesn't want to eat." Yet this was Tody trying to keep mom alive. Plus, she is a great cook! There was food for days! That being said, they had been with us for a month and their return flight home to Florida was fast approaching. They had made the decision, to return home even if mom had not yet passed. Understood! They'd had their time with her and been an enormous help.

Saturday morning, July 23rd, 2016, surrounded by family, she went to the city of gold. That was what she described to us almost daily during her last week on earth. *"A beautiful place with people in white robes and gold streets."* She died at ninety-one years of age, but very young at heart! She was gone. The woman that gave me so much, yet could be so infuriating. To me, she was a complicated woman and I had developed and accepted my own reasoning as to why, though I never expected to learn what may have been the largest reason for who she became, and created a dramatic turn altering our family unit.

With Tody living in Florida, we began to communicate by phone almost daily. We were filling the void of mom being gone and not being able to speak with her. Thoughts of my moving to Florida were far more prevalent and now in the forefront of my mind. The Minnesota winters were just not fun or enjoyable any longer and I hated the bundling up during the winter months and I really dislike being cold. My age was showing! UGH! In January of 2019, I knew I needed to leave. It felt impulsive, and it was! My home sold immediately. I called Tody and said *"My house just sold."* Her reply: *"Yippee! Get in your car and start driving!"* I worked right up until the day before I was to get on the road and begin the next chapter of my life. God only knows what that was going to be! I MUST be crazy! Starting over at sixty-three years of age. Somehow, I just didn't care. I wanted to live the rest of my life soaking in the warmth of sunshine, walking the beaches, and create a simple, quiet lifestyle for myself.

My son Russell flew home and spent a week with me packing up a truck with my belongings, then drove it down to Florida and put everything into storage for me. Plus, it gave him a few days to spend time with his cousin and Aunt Tody. I stayed with my brother, Kelley, and his wife Judy for a few days giving me time to be with them before I took off.

It's now Friday March 15th, 2019 and we spent the evening looking at photo's, reminiscing about life, our upbringing, memories we had, all that fun stuff, oddities, and some sad things of course, but all in all, how fortunate we were to have lived a simple uncomplicated life. But when the conversation turned to the relationship between our parents, Kelley brought up a memory he had since a small boy about our mother and the time she took him to California. I asked why would they have gone to California and was it only him? Where was Tody? Where was I? Was our brother Sean born yet? We were after all living in Minnesota. Why on earth would mother take Kelley to California alone? Where was daddy? Kelley said he didn't remember much, except getting on the airplane and throwing up into the barf bag (as we called them).

He remembered that to watch television in the motel room it needed to be fed quarters, and seeing a big turtle on the beach. He recalled our half-brother Gary being there with them but unclear if anyone else was there. WHAT did he just say?! As the conversation progressed, we decided Kelley must have been around two and a half – to three years old. So, either mom was pregnant with me or I had just been born. Our younger brother not on the scene yet. The timeline and time of year not established. I was full of questions, *"Then either I was not born yet or I was an infant meaning, I had to be with you because mom breast fed me for a year and a half, or wait ... if I was not born yet, were mom and Gary together? Like together, together? If you were only about three ... then, wait ... do you think I am Gary's daughter? Not daddy's?"*

Why that popped into my head I haven't a clue except this was all weird and I'm trying to put together a timeline. Of all my half siblings I was closest to Gary. Throughout my entire life he was always reaching out to me and wanting to know about my life, how were the kids, was I happy? Such a caring, attentive brother. Yet, the timing was right and Kelley looking at me, said nothing but the tilt of his head and glance of his eyes said, *"Maybe!"* Hmmmm!

End of discussion. Interesting but absurd! My imagination had gone wild. Mom would NEVER do anything of the sort. I rose the next morning and began my drive south. I planned to take my time driving allowing myself two weeks in Wisconsin with my oldest son, Adam, and my granddaughters, Julia and Abigail, while my daughter-in-law, Sarah was in Washington D.C. doing research for a project of hers. Boy, that will let you know you're not as young as you think you are when taking care of a two- and five-year-old! But what fun! My next stop would be in Chicago with my daughter, Madeline for a few days.

Now being alone, I had all the time in the world to once again think about what Kelley had said. There must have been others along on that trip. Mother wouldn't have done anything like run off, or have an affair with Gary. He was her stepson. Nope ... that just could not be the truth. She was our strait-laced, over protective mother. That's just absurd! I didn't give it another thought. Finally, April 3 found me in the glorious Florida weather at Tody's front door. Tody and I were having so much fun, and she included me in all of her social activities. She filled our days and evenings attending Bunco groups, Wine-Time, Junior League, History Club, Book Club, the Symphony and gatherings with friends. Once again, the comments on how we didn't look related or like sisters seemed to be happening everywhere we went. *"Wow, the two of you look nothing alike. I wouldn't guess you were sisters. Same parents?"* To which Tody was always quick to respond with *"Yes, we do have the same mom and dad!"* I would nod in agreement and we'd all have a chuckle! We would stay up late watching tv and laughing at the day's events. Bob was now in the later stages of dementia and he was declining rapidly. July 3rd, he went to Heaven. They really were a fabulous team for fifty years!

SCENE 2: WHAT BABY?

March 2020 brought news from Beverly Benham who had been married to our half-brother Daryl (Gary's brother) until his death in 2006 of Multiple Myeloma. Bev wrote to inform us she had now been diagnosed with dementia and wanted to get pictures to us before she would never be able to remember who might want them. Among the photos there were pictures of our mom as Mrs. Minnesota, Beverly's and Daryl's wedding in July of 1956, with one particular photo from their wedding catching my attention. I had seen this photo before among mother's things. It was a small picture of mom, Gary, Gary holding me when I was seven months old, and another woman. I never knew who the other woman was but Bev had written everyone's names on the back and it was Virtue. Oh my God! Gary's mother, Virtue! She had been daddy's second wife. Mom was daddy's fourth wife.

I stood there frozen for a moment. My head was racing with thoughts. Thoughts bouncing around in my head seeming to all speak loudly at the same time. I immediately thought why is mother the only one smiling and looking like the cat that ate the canary, while Gary looked miserable and his mom was looking at me. Why am I in this photo? Where were Tody, and Kelley? Why isn't Archie in this picture? He is after all Gary and Daryl's father and must have been at the wedding as well. NOW my gut reaction sensed something different and my thoughts immediately went back to the conversation I'd had with my brother Kelley a year earlier. Kelley being about three when he went to California with mom ... taking an airplane ... staying in a motel ... Perhaps there is more to this photo than any of us knew. Until now.

Was this a snapshot of me with possibly my family? With my paternal grandmother. Every nerve in my body was at attention. I decided it was time to approach the subject with Tody. We settled into the family room to relax for the evening and before long, the time seemed right to bring up how sweet it was of Beverly to send the photos which then prompted me to start reminiscing about our childhood, upbringing, mom and daddy, their personalities, marriage, relationship or lack of it, and *that* photo. I proceeded to tell her what Kelley said the last night I was with him and within seconds the color in Tody's face drained. Her expression frozen, her eyes wide and distant. A look of fear is what I saw. She became very serious, seeming to search for the right words and then quietly she said *"I can't believe Kelley spilled the beans."*

At this moment it was obvious to me, Tody and Kelley had spoken about this at other times in their lives. Never sharing that story with me because of what they suspected as small children. *"So, it's true? Kelley, mom and Gary were in California?"* I asked. She then told me she too was in California with mom, Gary, and Kelley. Well, now my interest is peaked. She knew. She *knows!* Tody suspected even at the young age of eight. Her instincts and intelligence imbedded the thought that there was an affair going on between mom and Gary.

Tody told me she remembered them all being in a motel room and she and Kelley were in one bed while Gary and mom were in the other. GEESH! I don't want to visualize that scenario! On the other hand, THAT explains a lot! I said, *"Ah ha, then they were having an affair and that must have been when mom had contemplated leaving our father Archie. Could I be Gary's daughter?"* I questioned.

Tody still staring at me, her eyes darting from side to side while nodding her head in a non-committal way, as if circular, and softly saying, *"I don't know. I don't 'really' know. Maybe."* But she recalled another time Gary and mom were being very playful with Gary throwing mother over his shoulder causing Tody to yell, *"Stop it. You'll hurt the baby."* Tody knew mom was pregnant. Was I that baby? Was there another baby? What baby?

O.K., that was all I needed. I knew at that moment there could be no sitting on this information for the rest of my life and that I would need to do some investigating. It was an adrenaline rush knowing there may be a past scandal to uncover. What's wrong with me?! This would change my family tree, as well as my children's. My curiosity peaked wondering what in the world has been going on! Tody had done the Ancestry.com DNA testing two years prior and had sent all of us the results in an email. They looked to be accurate as far as both our parent's heritage. Mom with her Finnish and Russian heritage and daddy's Irish, English, and Scottish. But now I have more questions. I told her I was going to send away for the same DNA kit and if there are any discrepancies between hers and mine, it may prove I have a different father.

I teasingly told Tody, *"Just think! We are sisters AND you may be my auntie! You'd be my sister-auntie!"* She tried to chuckle but her shoulders slumped, her eyes became moist with tears, and she said, *"I just want to be your sister. I don't want our family structure to be different."* We hugged and I said, *"We will always be sisters."*

The next morning, I ordered the test and then proceeded to call our brother Kelley. Explaining my conversation with Tody and what she recalled about that trip to California and that I just ordered the DNA test. I also sent an email to Beverly, thanking her for the pictures and flat out asking if Gary was my biological father? She, quite possibly, may be the only living relative that might have some answers for me, but she has dementia. Two days later, I received a voice message from Bev asking me to call her. I phoned her back immediately and luckily her daughter, Amber, my niece was with her.

It was Amber who seemed so sure that Gary was my father. I asked her if Kilyn my niece, and Gary and Judy's daughter, knew this could be a possibility. She wasn't sure. She told me she would text me the phone number of a Charles Shipman. He was a friend of Gary and Daryl's and he would be the one to fill in most of the story. My story. Shortly after our conversation I received this Facebook message from Amber:

Dear Dorothy, Mom has forgotten so much due to Alzheimer's, that she wasn't able to recall much from her wedding, etc. But she just called Charles Shipman, and he knows the whole story about you, your mom, and Gary! You ARE Gary's child, and possibly Kelley and Tody. I'm glad you can finally get some answers! Gary, Dad and Charles were best friends! Here is Charles' number: xxx-xxx-xxxx

WOW! I am grateful to have some insight prompting me to continue down the path of discovery. Finding the people who would be able to shed more light on the questions I have and who all knows the truth?

SCENE 3: WHO KNEW?

If this is true, the key players are no longer with us. Gary, his wife Judy, and Daryl are deceased. Mom passed in 2016. The question is does Kilyn know? **Does. Kilyn. Know?** Would she have been told that we were indeed sisters and not aunt and niece? Is Gary my biological father and not my half-brother? ... or in this case BOTH! Good grief! The two people that seem to have no doubt are Beverly, Amber and this Charles Shipman. After a delightful conversation with Amber, who was positive Gary was my father, I did ask them if they felt Kilyn had been told. They weren't sure but taking a good guess, and knowing Gary and Judy, they more than likely shared this information with her. I phoned Kilyn and left a voice message asking her to call me.

My next phone call would be to Charles Shipman. He picked up after one ring and the conversation began with stories of their escapades as young boy's and how they were all ruffians! Friends for life. Without hesitation he confirmed that *"100% you are Gary's daughter and I would stake my life on it. Not Archie's child. Your mom and Gary were very much in love but Gary was young."* Gary being twenty-two and mother thirty.

Gary was in the Army at this time and would need to provide for a wife and now three children, as mother would never have left Tody and Kelley with Archie. There wasn't any money, how would he support a family of five? They must have realized their plan to be together wouldn't work and returned to Minnesota. I wonder how they came to that conclusion and it must have been difficult making that decision. Was it Gary's decision or mother's? It may have been upon returning to Minnesota Tody recalled there being a meeting, a long meeting in another room with dad, mom and Gary. Charles confirmed that meeting as well. Perhaps this is when the altercation between Gary and Archie broke out. A fight Kelley, Tody, and Charles all remember. Gary and Archie having words when they started to throw fists. It ended up with Gary hitting him hard enough sending him backward onto a coffee table which shattered on impact.

Since Amber thought maybe Tody or Kelley might be Gary's children, I asked Charles and he said none of their names rang a bell, only mine and he has known that all along. I thanked Charles for the conversation and asked if I could call again after my DNA results came in, as I was sure to have more questions. He graciously said yes.

I wanted to keep Tody and Kelley informed on any information I was receiving and while Kelley and Judy were fine with it and understanding, with Tody I was met with a bit of hesitancy.

We first spoke on the phone and I told her that Amber and Bev confirmed that I was Gary's child. Her response was cool, yet sad with her saying she didn't want the structure of the family to change. But let's face it, it has possibly changed. Mine would change. Then I had an incoming call I needed to take and would get back to her. I did so in a text and copied and pasted Amber's message to me, for her to read. Now her response was more of anger and probably hurt. Perhaps the frustration of having kept that information bottled up for such a long time, and now the possibility she was correct all along. She did not want this exposed and felt Amber should not have put this into writing for anyone to find, even though it was a private message to me. But here's the deal ... this is my life. Shouldn't I be the devastated one?

This affects me, and my family, and my family history. My children deserve to know the truth and who is who in their family tree. My heart goes out to Tody as she wants no changes in our family structure and perhaps embarrassment to shadow mother or even our family. We are only human, have many faults and will continue to make many errors throughout our lives from which our greatest growth arises.

Through more conversation with Tody, she divulged the fact that grandma once asked her if she thought our mother was very smart. Tody also mentioned that when daddy was gone Gary would come into town. He and mom would leave for the day, saying they were going to a movie while grandma babysat. I don't think so! I know grandma knew better. Tody knew grandma knew better. Our grandma was no fool. Our mother was blatantly running around with her stepson and she didn't care. Now this makes me wonder if grandma shared this with Uncle Alan and did grandma talk to him about mother's escapades? He would make comments about how easily I tanned saying, *"Dorothy Kathleen, you walk outside and your skin absorbs the sun. You just tan so easily. Maybe it's because those gypsy's traveling through the towns in Finland were taking up with families!"* This was Uncle Alan's humor all the time so of course, it was a joke and we all would laugh. Or was it? Was it his way at hinting there was a reason for my being different than my siblings? Mother HAD to confide in someone.

I needed to approach Kilyn next. Did she know? She is Gary and Judy's daughter! Had they told her any of this? Sure enough, Kilyn confirmed that I was her dad's daughter and was more than happy to share any information her parents had told her. Kilyn proceeded to tell me that the day she and her mom were shopping for Kilyn's wedding invitations, they stopped for lunch and this is when her mom told her that the truth should always be told. Secrets not kept. Judy proceeded to inform Kilyn that I was not her aunt but in fact her sister. Gary was also my father. Kilyn said it was mind blowing and that it took her time to process this new information. DO YA THINK?! Absolutely!

Kilyn wasn't sure who all had been told and no one spoke of it. What Kilyn could confirm was that her parents were a real team, her mom was her best friend, and never lied to her. Eventually stating to me that my mom and her dad *"found comfort in one another at a time of need."* How beautiful is that? It all makes sense. This is why mother wanted Kilyn in my wedding. In her own way she was keeping Gary in the loop without divulging the truth to me. So here was my biological father standing in the wings watching his daughter be escorted down the aisle by another man, my step-father. It was dawning on me now that here he was never able to celebrate any of my accomplishments as my dad, but quietly and respectfully stood in the wings watching in his role as a proud half-brother.

The moments when I was in high school and voted Most Respected and crowned Home Coming Queen. Being crowned Miss America as he watched from his living room. Kilyn still remembers her dad, our dad, jumping up and down with excitement and crying with joy that I had won. Gary always made a point of calling me many times throughout the year to touch base and catch up on news. Unfortunately, he heard me complain about how frustrating mother was, her silent treatments, and when we were not having a relationship. I think that may have saddened him. I never gave his phone calls a second thought except as a brother who wanted to always stay connected. Those phone calls now have a much different meaning. I wonder how many times he wanted to tell me. Did he and mother think about or agree on a time they would tell me? Had he thought about telling me as he progressively became more ill with his heart condition? Even if he wanted to, I am sure he vowed to mother never to say anything. Respecting her wishes, he took this secret promise to his grave out of respect to mother.

SCENE 4: DNA

Independently Kilyn and Tody had both participated in the Ancestry DNA testing. I'd sent mine in and would need to wait about eight weeks. I should be matched up to theirs and who knows who else. April 22nd my results arrived and sure enough it matched me up to Tody and Kilyn with almost the same amount of cm's (whatever those are) and there, directly underneath their names was Teddy Mattson. It would not be possible to be a blood relation to him unless Gary was my biological father and Virtue, my grandmother.

Teddy is one of Virtue's sons from her second marriage and Gary's half-brother. There wasn't a doubt now that Kilyn was my sister and Gary my father. But a second more in-depth test could solidify this information. I decided to ask Kilyn if she would do another DNA test with me. A more thorough sibling's test to which she agreed. I ordered it through a clinic and the kits were mailed to us that day. Once the clinic received them, it would only take three days for a confirmation.

On May 1st, 2020, as I was getting ready for bed, I saw there was a new email that had just came in. The in-depth, clinical DNA study. The results confirmed 99.9% we were half siblings. I sent the email immediately to Kilyn. She began sending me our father's photos, papers of interest, and it began our beautiful new relationship.

I shared this new found information with my younger brother Sean and suggested if he had any doubts as to who his father may be, he too should do the DNA test through Ancestry. So far he hasn't. Then my children. They had a new grandfather and great grandmother. They of course, were all surprised and trying to make heads and tails of it as I explained how this happened. Their reaction being, *"WHAT? WHOA! WHAT? This is crazy!"* Prompting my son Russell to ask, ***"Wait ... I am your son, right?"*** HA! We had a good laugh over that and I assured all of them they did know who their fathers were. But their lovely reaction and question for me was ***"How are you, mom?"***

So, I have my answer. Gary is my biological father. Now what? What do I do with this information? I still have so many questions. When did the affair between mom and Gary begin? My goodness ... she knew him as a child. When did feelings change from parent-child to lovers? Eeew, who does that? Who initiated THAT first encounter and HOW?

My mother was older and I'm just going to put it on her! When did it end? I found a picture in my scrapbook that on the back mother wrote *"Darling~ Here is our beautiful daughter looking her best for you. We love you very much. Dorothy Kathleen, 14 months old Feb. 1957."* There is no way she would have written this to Archie. Did my mother instigate the one and only 'family' photo with all of us? Did they sneak off and have the photographer take the photo without others knowing? Giving them one little snapshot of us as a family. Me, my parent's and paternal grandmother! What did mother say or could she say to Virtue? *"Gee Virtue, I slept with your son, who as you know is my stepson, we have given you your first grandchild even though I'm currently married to your ex-husband who mis-treated you. Unfortunately, Virtue, this must be kept secret and you can have no contact with your granddaughter."* Poor Virtue. Has anyone thought about poor Virtue and what she was going through? What a soap-opera! But this is reality. It happened and there is no changing the past. It is what it is and all we can do is deal with the facts. It's the same scenario that has played out for centuries. Really, it's nothing new. It's called life and it just happened to play out in my life.

My heart goes out to all involved. To Judy, dear, dear, sweet Judy. Who because of her love for her husband, Gary, upheld his and mother's secret. She always welcomed me into her home with love. To Gary ... who was never allowed to claim me as his own or know my children, his grandchildren. He cheered me on from the wings and kept silent. My grandmother Virtue. I can only imagine she was probably in shock! Let's just repeat this again...*Her first born son had an affair with the woman who was the current and fourth wife of her ex-husband, giving birth to her first grandchild.* Did her current husband know? She must have confided in him. They had five-year-old twins at home at the time of my birth and still trying to make a new home-life for herself. She went on to have two more sons after my birth. I often think how lovely it would have been to know Virtue and if we shared any similar traits, likes and dislikes. What may I have inherited from her other than now being Norwegian?

To my mother; It would have been nice to hear what happened from your lips. Did you ever contemplate telling me before you died? Did the two of you ever speak about telling me once I reached the age of, let's say, twenty-one? Or because, at the age of twenty, when I became Miss America, it definitely would not have been the right time possibly leaking to the press and been presented to the public as a scandal? Bringing unwanted attention to all of us. Were you protecting me or were you protecting yourself? Yet I wonder if you would have been capable of telling the whole truth or making it fit your reality. Were you afraid to tell me? Had enough time passed where you believed it didn't matter? I would never have wanted you to feel shame for finding love at one time. But I am sad you had to relinquish it only to live with a man you did not love. How many times was your heart breaking through the years? Mine breaks thinking about it. I do wonder how different my life would have been growing up with Gary and knowing him as my dad, but what an affect that would have had on my older siblings. I was happy when you found O.B. and lived a fun life filled with music and dancing while in a loving marriage.

Over the last year, I've read numerous autobiographies with the same story line learning that the authors were devastated. I am not devastated. Is there something wrong with me? There must be something wrong with me. I have questioned this many, many times but I don't think so. I haven't felt the need for therapy over this and have always believed that every person has their own path in life and we either cope with what is presented to us and move on or we become stuck. I have never wanted to feel stuck in life. I have always been ready for the next segment or chapter that may be around the corner. I will say life hasn't been dull. It has been exhausting at times, but I wouldn't change much given the chance. I embrace the life given to me so filled with laughter, heartbreak, color and characters. Perhaps it's the theater-side of me that finds all of this rather fascinating.

As I wrote this over the last year, many people have said how therapeutic it must be. It hasn't been. I have re-lived events and emotions I didn't want to, but with that said, hopefully those have been put to bed for good now. I've questioned whether I should continue writing many times, only to begin again the next day like it was calling to me. I told my sister, Tody, I think it's mom calling from up above. Directing and orchestrating all these revelations coming to light at this time in my life, wanting me to now learn the truth and write about it. WHY? Because it gives her one more chance at fame and being known! Even from the grave! Her one last hurrah! And in Tody's words, *"SHE'S BAAACK!"*

So, let's do a quick re-cap of who I am in my family tree.

My father is now my grandfather. My brother is now my father. His brother is now my uncle. My sister is my sister-auntie and my brothers are now my brother-uncles. My nieces have become my first cousins with the exception of Kilyn, who is now my sister. Nephews are now my cousins. My first cousins on my mother's side are still first cousins and now that Virtue is my grandmother, I have a whole new limb on my tree! But hey, I'm still a Benham and mom is still mom! There! That clears it all up!!

The definition of a bastard child according to Merriam-Webster is;

1: of illegitimate birth: bastard. 2 outwardly similar or corresponding to something without having its genuine qualities; false the spurious eminence of the pop celebrity. 3a: of falsified of erroneously attributed origin: forged. B: of deceitful nature or quality spurious excuses.

More results:

Who is considered a bastard child? A person born of parents not married to each other; illegitimate child. Noun. The definition of a bastard is someone whose parents did not marry, or is something that has been changed or is not normal. Or is slang for someone who people do not like.

Well, I find the word 'spurious' fascinating, and 'not normal' alright with me. We all have a façade we put on at times in public, trying to create the semblance of perfection. There's that word again. Are any of us *normal*? That could be boring. It *would* be boring. I await with great anticipation the next chapter in my life. With Sisu, I will head directly into that spot light with love for my family and perhaps not so many more surprises! This was a big one and I proudly claim my right as the Bastard Queen!

CHEERS!

Mother, Gary, Me at 7 months, Virtue

Gary Benham

My Biological Father

Gary Benham - Older

Gary Benham, Daryl Benham, Charles Shipman

Tody and Me

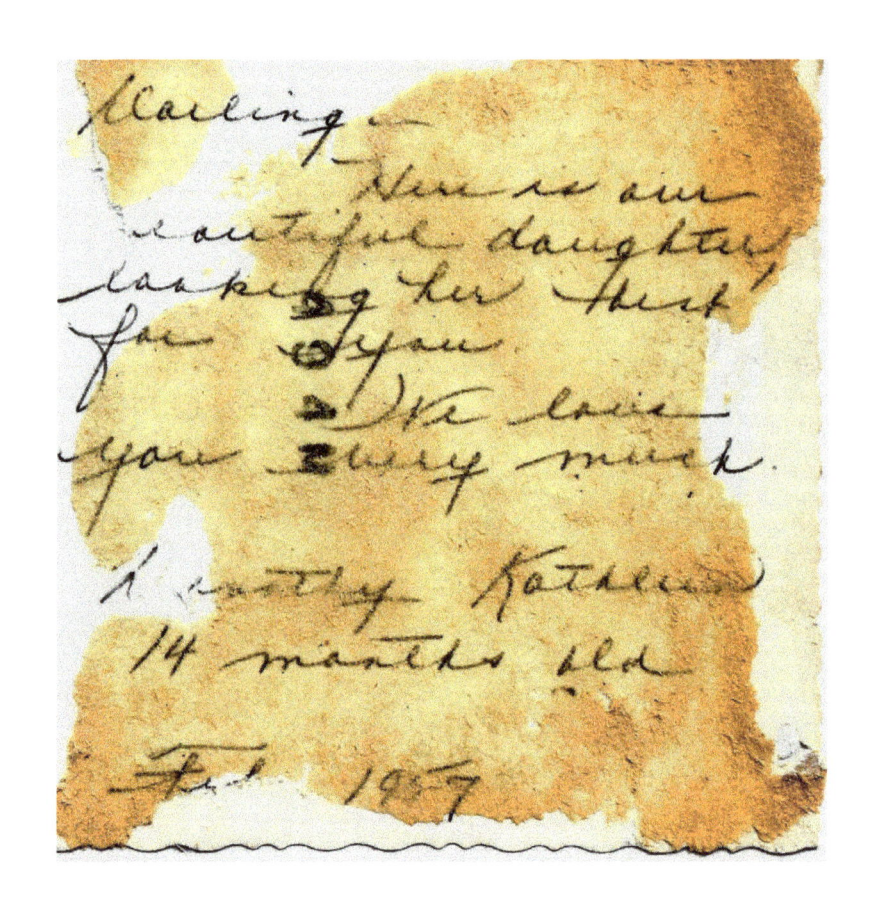

Writing on Back of Old Photo

Mom gave to Gary

Front of Photo with Writing on Back

Christmas 2015 with my Children

My Four Grandkids in 2018

Max, Abigail, Julia, and Blake

Julia, Abigail, and Me

Archibald Benham

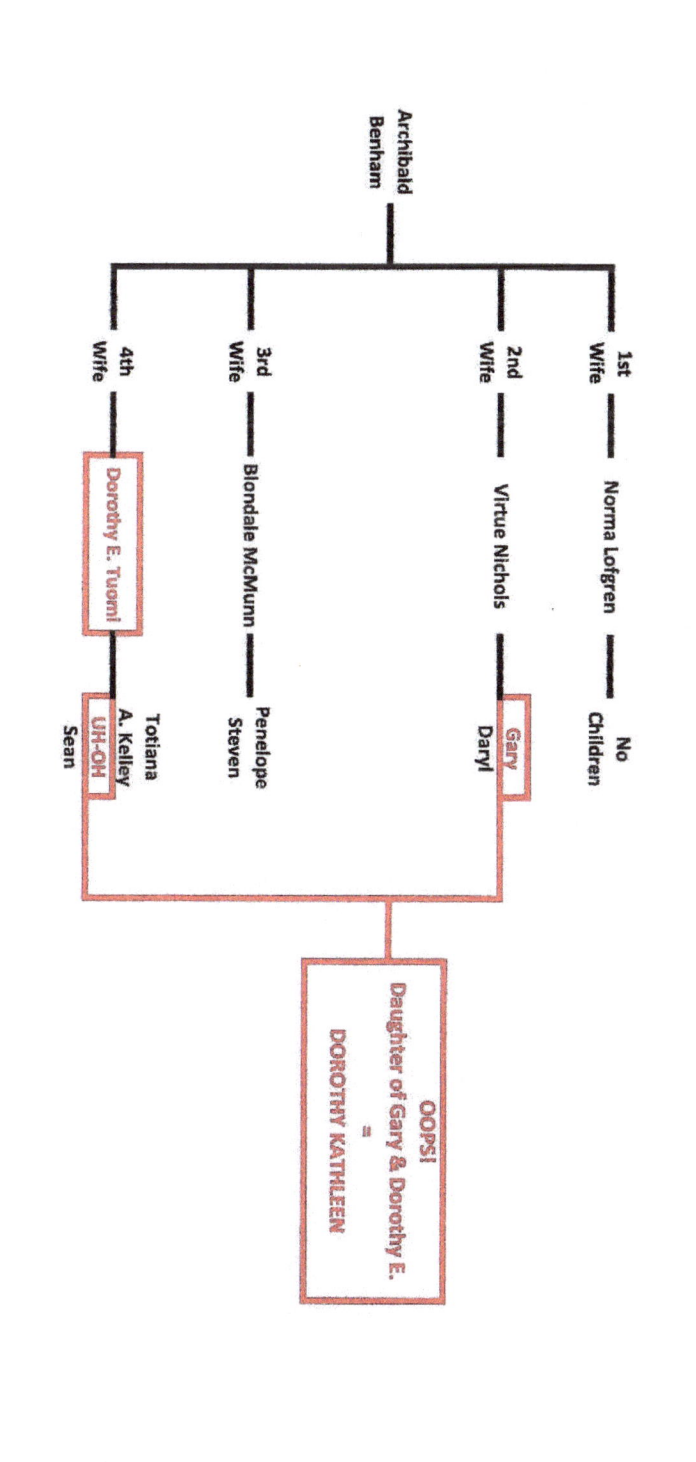

- **1st Wife** — Norma Lofgren — No Children
- **2nd Wife** — Virtue Nichols
  - Gary
  - Daryl
- **3rd Wife** — Blondale McMunn
  - Penelope
  - Steven
- **4th Wife** — Dorothy E. Tuomi
  - Totiana A. Kelley **UH-OH**
  - Sean

OOPS!
Daughter of Gary & Dorothy E.
=
DOROTHY KATHLEEN

ABOUT THE AUTHOR

Photo Credit: Donald B. Kravitz / DBKphoto

Dorothy Benham, Miss America 1977, is a classically trained lyric-coloratura soprano having performed in concert with Symphony Orchestras, Opera companies, and an original cast member of the Tony and Grammy Award-winning Broadway show *Jerome Robbins' Broadway* where she was featured as the "Somewhere" soloist and part of the ensemble. She sang the National Anthem for the 1979 World Series games in Pittsburgh, PA., and at a fundraiser for President Reagan, then for the Sammy Davis Jr. Celebrity Dinner. In 1976 Dorothy was the featured half time performer at the Liberty Bowl. She performed with Bob Hope and Doc Severinsen, and was chosen by Peter Schickele (aka PDQ Bach) as the soprano for his composer showcase at the Lincoln Center in NYC. She has been a frequent guest soloist on *The Hour of Power* in Garden Grove, California, and was honored to sing for their final Christmas Eve Service 2012 and then again for the final Sunday worship service at the Crystal Cathedral June 30th, 2013.

Following her year as Miss America, Dorothy not only was a featured performer, co-host and judge of the Miss America Pageant, but worked extensively in television and radio as a spokesperson for a variety of companies.

Dorothy's USO work began with the Miss America USO Troupe performing for our Servicemen in Japan, Korea, the Philippines and Guam. In 1981 she was the Host and performer for the USO's 40th Anniversary Celebration in Stuttgart, Germany. Then along with Brooke Shields and the USO performed aboard the USS John F. Kennedy at the 1986 Statue of Liberty Bi-Centennial Celebration for President and Mrs. Reagan.

Dorothy is the proud mother of six children and seven grandchildren.

CPSIA information can be obtained
at www.ICGtesting.com
Printed in the USA
BVHW022052240821
615133BV00004B/260